BONDS OF AFFECTION
Thoreau on Dogs and Cats

Bonds of Affection

THOREAU ON DOGS AND CATS

Edited by Wesley T. Mott

Foreword by Elizabeth Marshall Thomas

Engravings by Barry Moser

UNIVERSITY OF MASSACHUSETTS PRESS

AMHERST & BOSTON

Published in cooperation with

THE THOREAU SOCIETY

Copyright © 2005 by The Thoreau Society
Foreword © 2005 by Elizabeth Marshall Thomas
All rights reserved
Printed in the United States of America
LC 2005005405
ISBN 1-55849-499-5 (library cloth ed.); 498-7 (paper)

Set in Monotype Bell
Printed on recycled paper by Thomson-Shore, Inc.

Library of Congress Cataloging-in-Publication Data

Thoreau, Henry David, 1817–1862.
Bonds of affection : Thoreau on dogs and cats / edited by Wesley T. Mott ;
foreword by Elizabeth Marshall Thomas.
    p. cm. — (The spirit of Thoreau series)
    Includes bibliographical references (p.   ).
    ISBN 1-55849-498-7 (pbk. : alk. paper) —
    ISBN 1-55849-499-5 (library cloth : alk. paper)
    1. Thoreau, Henry David, 1817–1862—Quotations.
    2. Human-animal relationships—Quotations, maxims, etc.
3. Dogs—Quotations, maxims, etc. 4. Cats—Quotations, maxims, etc.
I. Title: Thoreau on dogs and cats. II. Mott, Wesley T. III. Title
IV. Series: Thoreau, Henry David, 1817–1862. Spirit of Thoreau.

PS3042.M64 2005
818'.309—dc22
2005005405

British Library Cataloguing in Publication data are available.

For my grandchildren
Morgan, Quinn, Ben, and Julia
and the animals with whom they will share
bonds of affection

Every one experiences that while his relation to another actually may be one of distrust & disappointment he may still have relations to him ideally & so really—in spite of both[.] He is faintly conscious of a confidence & satisfaction somewhere. & all further intercourse is based on this experience of success[.]

The very dogs & cats incline to affection in their relation to man. It often happens that a man is more humanely related to a cat or dog than to any human being. What bond is it relates us to any animal we keep in the house but the bond of affection. In a degree we grow to love one another.

29 April 1851, Journal *3:210*

The necessaries of life for man in this climate may, accurately enough, be distributed under the several heads of Food, Shelter, Clothing, and Fuel; for not till we have secured these are we prepared to entertain the true problems of life with freedom and a prospect of success. Man has invented, not only houses, but clothes and cooked food; and possibly from the accidental discovery of the warmth of fire, and the consequent use of it, at first a luxury, arose the present necessity to sit by it. We observe cats and dogs acquiring the same second nature.

"Economy," Walden, *12*

CONTENTS

FOREWORD

ELIZABETH MARSHALL THOMAS

WHY ARE DOGS AND CATS so important to us? No answer can be simple, not only because the dog and the cat each took its own path from the wild to our households today, but also because the element that we human beings bring to the situation is older than our species.

While our ancestors in glacial times were moving northward from the sites of our African origins onto the Eurasian steppe—the cold-climate version of our homeland savannah—their arrival was surely noted by all the resident species. Some of them, the wolves, must have seen certain similarities between themselves and the newcomers. For instance, both the wolves and the people had helpless infants who, unlike many other animals, could not survive out in the open but needed to be kept in shelters. The wolves made dens, and the people sought out caves. Perhaps the wolves also noticed that, like themselves, the people hunted in groups for big game—often for the very same animals. Both wolves and people brought meat home to their dens or shelters. But here was an important difference: The people carried the meat home in their hands or on their backs, to cook and eat it in a lengthy operation that took place above ground in view of any observer. The wolves, in contrast, carried food home hidden in their stomachs, to be heaved up for the pups in a maneuver that took place quickly at the mouth of the concealing den. The eating method of the people was obvious to the wolves, but not vice versa.

Especially in winter, when all those who lived by hunting had a very hard time finding enough food to keep their souls within their bodies, the smell of cooking meat must have carried far on the cold wind, and the sight of people eating must have been very compelling to the wolves, who would have responded by lurking around the camps of the people. The wolves would have learned the ways of the people soon enough and would have followed hunting parties, hoping to snatch a bite of the victim or at least to eat the bloody snow after the human hunters had taken their kill and left the area.

Then what? Wolves were themselves cooperative hunters, so perhaps they helped the people by driving their victims toward them, in the manner of herding dogs. Or perhaps they showed the people where their victims were hiding, in the manner of bird dogs. Wolves herd game, and they also point, bird-dog style, as a way of communicating with each other—perhaps it wasn't too great a leap for them to do the same for our species. Perhaps the people rewarded the helpful wolves, although that doesn't seem too likely; perhaps the wolves simply hoped to snatch a share of the meat before the people took over the entire carcass.

What mattered to the wolves was that they became scavengers at the people's camps. Even if the people didn't feed them (if the Paleolithic hunters were anything like modern hunter/gatherers, they didn't feed animals), at least the wolves could help themselves to the scraps. Archaeologists have found fossilized wolf scats in Paleolithic camps, showing that the people had a tolerant attitude toward the presence of wolves, and also toward their lack of housebreaking skills. Perhaps the presence of a few scats seemed a small price to pay for the fact that if wolves were in or around the camp, they would warn the people of other predators who were drawn to the piles of meat resulting from successful hunts. If wolves gave warnings, they would have been warning one another, but the people would benefit too, and would then be more likely to tolerate the wolves.

The wild wolves were big animals. The bigger they were, the better they could withstand the Paleolithic winter, and the better they could overcome their prey. But when wolves became scavengers, first in Paleolithic camps, later in Neolithic villages, they found themselves trying to survive on extremely small amounts of food—a scrap of skin here, a discarded bone fragment there—so large size became a disadvantage. Early on, the wolves who were becoming dogs seemed to settle on a proper phenotype—about forty pounds, a rangy body—that is still the phenotype of Third and Fourth World village dogs today and is the phenotype to which dogs revert when their living conditions leave them free to choose their own mates.

After we human beings became agriculturalists, we began to see advantages in certain traits exhibited by our wolf/dog colleagues, and began to try to control their breeding hoping to shape them into the useful servants that they are today, but all this was late in the process of domestication. The important part of the process happened much earlier, when the wolves saw advantages to life among us and took the opportunity. Today dogs and people are almost fused together. Dogs started it.

🐾   🐾   🐾

About 20,000 years later, cats did likewise. But whereas the dogs gave up their way of life to join us, the cats came to us along with most of their former ecosystem. The process began, interestingly enough, with the domestication of grass. The edible seeds borne by grasses don't deteriorate like most fruits and vegetables but can be stored almost indefinitely. When people realized this they began to keep quantities of grass seeds (by then known as grain) in containers against times of hunger. In the wild, however, these grass seeds were the foods of mice and rats, and when the people began to store the seeds in granaries, the mice and rats came in after them. Right behind the mice and rats came their predators, the small tabby wildcats, *Felis sylvestris lybica.* This little ecosystem—the grass seeds, the mice and rats, and the cats—is still with us today, virtually intact. The grass became the wheat and wheatlike grains that provide so much of our diet, while the Near Eastern mice became our ordinary house mice, the Near Eastern rats became the so-called Norway rats (who have nothing to do with Norway, despite the name), and the little wild cats became our house cats, *Felis sylvestris catus.*

The ways of the wildcats must have seemed agreeable to the people—the cats were clean and quiet, and they didn't steal human food, or at least, they didn't steal grain-based foods as the village dogs most certainly were doing, every chance they got. Instead, the cats protected human food by keeping the granaries relatively mouse-free. What more can one ask from a small wild animal? Perhaps the Egyptians were the only culture that deified cats, but other peoples certainly favored them highly, and carried them with them as they traveled the world.

Eight thousand years later, the domestic cats are much more like their wild cousins than dogs are like wolves, partly because their time with us has been shorter, and partly because neither their food nor their habits have changed. Then too, we interfere much less with the breeding of cats than with dogs, so that even today, many cats still choose their own mates. This alone accounts for the fact that cats live much longer than dogs, and lack the many disabilities that afflict dogs—disabilities such as hip dysplasia, deafness, skin diseases, and the like, all resulting from the arrogant human assumption that we know better than Gaia how dogs should reproduce. As more and more cat breeders try for flat faces, skeletal bodies, twisted fur, and other abnormalities that win them prizes in cat shows, cats will deteriorate also. But as long as cats are free to choose their own mates, they will remain close to their wild ancestors, which means that they will continue to live much longer than dogs, and in much better health. We have learned something about animal husbandry since the Neolithic, but Gaia knows much more.

❦   ❦   ❦

So dogs came to us in the Paleolithic, and cats in the Neolithic, and today, of course, neither animal still serves its original function—far from it. Leopards no longer creep up on us, and mice make only minor incursions on our food supply. We continue with our dog/cat relationships for reasons that no longer reflect why these animals joined us, but that come from our own deep past. Our reasons go back five million years to the Pleistocene, when climate change forced our ape ancestors out of the dwindling central African rain forests and made them into hunter/gatherers of the expanding, dry savannah. Water was scarce and food plants grew sparsely, and the little family bands of our ancestors, camped within walking distance of a water source, could not number more than fifteen or twenty people. More, the land would not support. The people depended on one another, and their bonds of unity had to remain very strong. In this form—small groups of extended families—we evolved our way through a succession of hominids until we emerged 150,000 years ago as *Homo sapiens,* but the pressures of our environment, and therefore the size of our groups, changed very little along the way. Whether we were *Australopithecus* or *Homo erectus,* we still had to make do with the food and drink of the savannah, in quantities and qualities that were determined by forces far beyond ourselves. In other words, the savannah doesn't support large populations of anything, or not in one place in the dry season.

By now, of course, our economic situation has dramatically changed, but the habits we developed during five million years on the savannah, with our relatives close by, are not easily shed.

In the few thousand years since we planted our first crops—
an act that soon led to the industrial revolution, urban envi-
ronments, and space travel—our emotional needs continue
unchanged while the size and structure of our groups have
changed profoundly. We no longer live among our kinfolks. We
are alone while in crowds because the crowds are made up of
strangers. We sense our isolation even if we don't see it. But
as our social system changed and a dangerous void appeared,
the dogs and cats stepped in to meet our modern needs with
the same ability that in earlier times they lent us their hunting
talents.

As for me, I live in a rural setting and my office is in a small
but rambling barn. With me are my dogs and cats. They can
come and go as they please through a dog door, but they feel as
close to me as I to them, so we spend our days together. But the
building is old and my office is porous, and at night, mice and
rats come in to take the food I have provided for my two parrots.
I don't think this poses much danger to the parrots, because
their large cages have high perches, and anyway, a parrot can
bite through a broomstick. Still, the parrots need their sleep,
and the mice and rats are so intelligent that traps are virtually useless, so I leave either the dogs or the cats behind when
I return to the house. Like the cats of the Neolithic granaries,
my cats do a good job with the mice, but the big rats have them
intimidated. Sometimes when I enter my office in the morning,
I find the parrot food gone and the cats hiding high up on the
bookshelves behind the books, peering out fearfully but also
very glad to see me. I know then that the rats are ganging up
on them, so the next night I exchange the cats with the dogs
so that the cats come back to the house and the dogs stay in
the office. After such a night I occasionally find a big rat dead
on the floor and I know the dogs have done their duty. Mostly,
though, I merely find leftover food in the parrots' dishes. As

the Paleolithic wolves kept the predators out of the caves of our ancestors, so my dogs keep the rats out of the office. Evidently, the rats take a good look through the rat hole before entering the room, and if they realize that the dogs are waiting for them, they decide to stay in the walls.

INTRODUCTION
Inclining to Affection
WESLEY T. MOTT

ONE EVENING IN THE WOODS, Henry David Thoreau wrote with famous extravagance in *Walden*, "I caught a glimpse of a woodchuck stealing across my path, and felt a strange thrill of savage delight, and was strongly tempted to seize and devour him raw; not that I was hungry then, except for that wildness which he represented. . . . I love the wild not less than the good" (210). Toward the end of *Walden* he declares that access to the woods and its creatures is an essential complement—even an antidote—to our civilized lives, and crucial to our health: "Our village life would stagnate if it were not for the unexplored forests and meadows which surround it. We need the tonic of wildness. . . . [W]e require that all things be mysterious and unexplorable, that land and sea be infinitely wild, unsurveyed and unfathomed by us because unfathomable. We can never have enough of Nature. . . . We need to witness our own limits transgressed, and some life pasturing freely where we never wander" (317–18).

Because untamed nature and its creatures viscerally remind Thoreau of his own animal nature, many of his readers are surprised to discover that he also wrote extensively about domestic animals—especially dogs and cats. Thoreau could be demanding of human friendships, which often seemed to him to fall short of expectations. Yet in his journal for 29 April 1851 he described with unabashed tenderness the emotional bond—the love—that *mutually* attracts people and their pets: "The very dogs & cats incline to affection in their relation to man. It often happens that a man is more humanely related to a cat or dog than to any human being. What bond is it relates us to any animal we keep in the house but the bond of affection. In a degree we grow to love one another."

The bonds between humans and domesticated animals are, of course, ancient, even prehistoric. Dogs were "the first animals to take up residence with people," explains Marion Schwartz, "and the only animals found in human societies all over the world"—a relationship dating back 12,000 years. Dogs are thus "a product of culture." The Asians who first arrived in what became the Americas brought dogs, and among Native Americans, dogs were "the only animal allied with humans" (2). In a terrible reversal of this relationship, conquistadors seeking to subdue the New World used mastiffs and greyhounds to terrify and attack native peoples (162). Sketchy evidence suggests that the more elusive cat may have first chosen to live with humans in the Middle East sometime between 7,000 and 11,000 years ago; certainly they became established—even venerated—in Egyptian agricultural society around 4000 B.C. But in the western hemisphere, the domestic cat is a much more recent arrival than the dog. Several kinds of felines are native to the Americas, according to Bruce Fogle, but what we know as the domestic cat probably derives from the African wildcat (*Encyclopedia of the Cat*, 19). Cats arrived with the earliest French, Dutch, and English settlers, including "at least one" aboard the *Mayflower*, and several were brought to Pennsylvania in the eighteenth century "to control a plague of rodents" (160, 24).

Countless coffee-table books are replete with anecdotes about the special fondness with which famous men and women through the ages have regarded their dogs and cats. Yet not until Henry Thoreau's age did humane treatment—let alone sentimental regard—of domestic animals become widespread.

Introduction

The eighteenth-century engravings of William Hogarth are just one example of the brutality facing dogs and cats in everyday life, a condition that English writers such as Alexander Pope and Samuel Johnson decried. In modern Europe, the dog gradually emerged more quickly than the cat as a companion to be valued and sometimes even cherished. This bias is evident in Edward Topsell's translation of Conrad Gesner's *The History of Four-footed Beasts* (London, 1607), a work Thoreau admired as an early attempt to classify and describe animals and, even more, as a work of imagination. Topsell has a six-page section "Of the Dog in general" in which he notes that, although certain negative human traits are associated with dogs, "[t]here is not any creature without reason, more loving to his Master, nor more serviceable . . . then is a Dog" (111). He goes on to spend thirty-five more pages describing different kinds of dogs, including their special traits and uses. By comparison, Topsell devotes barely four pages to a section "Of the Cat." With a show of objectivity he sketches the cat in history, lore, natural science, and different cultures; but his account is filled with superstition: He accepts the popular notion that cats are "the familiars of Witches" and that the brain and teeth of the cat are "venomous" (83), and he offers the bizarre recommendation that cats be used for various medicinal purposes. "The nature of this beast is, to love the place of her breeding, neither will she tarry in any strange place, although carryed far, being never willing to forsake the house, for the love of any man, and most contrary to the nature of a Dog, who will travaile abroad with his master" (82). The judgmental quality in Topsell's comparison of dogs and cats lingered well into the eighteenth century, notwithstanding exceptions such as the celebrated verse of the eccentric Christopher Smart for his beloved cat Jeoffry ("For he is of the tribe of tiger"). Even the great philosopher of sentiment, the Earl of Shaftesbury—who stressed the importance of affections to the moral sense and generally encouraged humane treatment of animals—had no use for cats. In his influential *Characteristics* (1711), he cautioned that excessive or misplaced affection signaled a depraved society, and he was appalled "that in some countries even monkeys, cats, crocodiles, and other vile or destructive animals have been esteemed holy, and worshipped even as deities" (1:254).

Despite the long history of companionship and practical service to humans by dogs and cats, it was not until the nineteenth century that a sea change in popular attitudes toward pets emerged in Europe and the United States—a change coincident with the rise of the middle class and the heightened significance attached to the home and domestic values and the elevation of the status of children. The home was regarded, on these shores, as a laboratory for the virtues necessary in a growing democratic nation and its rapidly expanding economy. The Romantic movement, moreover, had fed the concept of childhood as not simply a period of adulthood in miniature but as a passage in which knowledge, feeling, and independence should be fostered—a process that also enhanced the role of mothers. These values meshed with a key tenet of Transcendentalism—that each individual has dignity and worth. This conviction underlay the many reform movements of the 1840s and 1850s—abolition, women's rights, temperance, dietary reform, and reform of countless institutions—educational, political, penal, and those treating the blind, the deaf, and the mentally ill. For many reformers, the principle that all people are worthy of respect, and that cultivation of their well-being was both a personal and a social matter, extended to animal rights as well. Indeed, the condition and role of pets frequently were viewed as intertwined with other reforms. Educating the minds and hearts of youth was widely regarded as the best means to instill and nurture values and habits crucial to citizenship, and for some writers of children's books, no better means existed to reach the minds and hearts of youth than pets. The most influential of these writers was Eliza Lee (Cabot) Follen (1787–1860). Though neither a Concordian nor primarily a Transcendentalist, Mrs. Follen was an older contemporary of Thoreau, a liberal Unitarian, an abolitionist, and a prolific author of domestic fiction and children's literature. In *True Stories About Dogs and Cats* (1855), the narrator—the widow Mary Chilton—tells her boys, Harry and Frank, accounts of animals going through various trials to teach young readers lessons in loyalty, courage, and gentleness. The boys, like Follen's intended audience, are attentive and responsive, and they are moved to think and feel more widely about all creatures. One canine story elicits this reaction: "'Hurrah for dogs!' cried Harry, clapping his hands. 'I say they are as good as men any day. They say, Mother, that the Indians believe their dogs will go to heaven with them. Will they, Mother.'" Mrs. Chilton admits that "We know nothing of the future state of animals. . . . We only know that they are more gentle and intelligent the more kind we are to them" (13). This knowledge entails ethical responsibility: "You never know how intelligent an animal is till you treat it with kindness. All animals are easily frightened by human beings, and fear makes them stupid. Children naturally love animals, but sometimes a foolish boy loves to show his power over them, and so learns to be cruel" (18). Mrs. Follen carefully avoids patronizing sentimentality by stressing that children and animals mutually cultivate one another's best instincts.

Mrs. Chilton next challenges that bias lingering since Topsell's age, declaring, "I must say something in favor of the much-abused cat. Doubtless she would be a much better member of society, if she were better treated, if she had a better example set before her" (25). "Sportsmen," she observes, resent cats for catching birds. But we would do well, Mrs. Chilton argues, to acknowledge that cats and hunters exhibit *similar* behavior. Moreover, "'Men, women, and boys and girls are often cruel and unreasonable, not merely cats. The cat is as good as she knows how to be.' 'So you are, pussy,' said Harry, taking up his pet cat in his lap, and stroking her" (27). The boys get the message, which is reinforced by accounts of feline loyalty—of a cat who "flew violently" at a mother who tried to strike a child (37), of a cat who, after keeping vigil with its ill little owner, dies immediately after she does (40–41). Our relationship to cats, Mrs. Chilton concludes, is potentially spiritual as well as moral: "Does not the fact that love and kindness can make such an irritable animal as the cat so loving and grateful, teach us all their heavenly power? Ought we not to do all which we can to bring out this better nature? . . . I therefore am the friend of the poor, despised, abused, neglected, suspected, calumniated cat" (41–42).

Mrs. Chilton goes on to tell anecdotes from history and from other cultures. Then, in a shocking twist, she reveals that the ethical treatment of animals is not simply a domestic matter or mere child's play. "I grieve to say," Mrs. Chilton suddenly declares, "that, here in this civilized land, blood-hounds are sometimes used to catch runaway slaves" (58), and she cites the recent Anthony Burns case as an example of this horror. Nurtured on the kind treatment of animals, the boys are prepared to grasp the fact of immorality and cruelty in the human realm. Frank responds, "O, it is very wicked, Mother!" "So I think, Frank," his mother replies; "let us hope that the time will come when every man and woman and child in our land will think so, and then there will be no more slaves" (59). Implicit in Mrs. Chilton's hope is Mrs. Follen's conviction that even in children's literature the kinder treatment of animals not only could redeem the home but also, by shaping young hearts and minds, powerfully serve to ameliorate terrible social evils as well.

Domestic animals were important in the households and writings of the major Concord authors. Louisa May Alcott—the greatest author of domestic fiction and "the Children's Friend"—was interested in reform but was rarely as overtly didactic as Mrs. Follen. Frequently, however, she placed cats in her fictional homes as a barometer of the decency and sensitivity of her human characters. As Katharine M. Rogers has astutely written, "Alcott was so intent on establishing the connection between cat and home that she associated cats with the good little girls of her fiction more than with the unconventional women who represent herself, even though she was, in fact, passionately fond of cats. It is not Jo but gentle, domestic Beth who is particularly devoted to the March family cats in *Little Women* (1868)" (102). Beth grows catnip for the family's kittens and is most expressive of her feelings toward them, but the disappearance of the Marches' beloved Mrs. Snowball Pat Paw also elicits from Jo a notice of "Public Bereavement" and a verse "Lament" in the girls' inhouse newspaper, *The Pickwick Portfolio*.

The Alcotts' near neighbor Ralph Waldo Emerson was habitually more aloof from household pets. "He respected and praised the useful domestic animals" from a distance, his son Edward wrote, and he particularly admired horses. But "[p]et animals he cared nothing for and shrank from touching them, though he admired the beauty and grace of cats" (Edward Waldo Emerson, *Emerson in Concord*, 158, 159). Waldo included one anecdote of a family cat's bad behavior—and his younger daughter's reaction—in the local news he sent on 20 July 1843 to Thoreau, who was then on Staten Island: "Edith & Ellen are in high health, and as pussy has this afternoon nearly killed a young oriole, Edie tells all comers with great energy her one story, 'Birdy—sick'" (*Letters* 7:551). Once a journalist writing an article on the canine friends of "Authors and Statesmen" asked Edward for "anecdotes showing my father's liking for dogs." The son could only come up with the memory of Waldo's "delight and sympathy" in reading "to his family, how when the Rev. Sydney Smith was asked by a lady for a motto to be engraved on the collar of her little dog Spot, the divine suggested the line from Macbeth, 'Out! damnèd Spot!'" (*Emerson in Concord*, 159).

Lidian Emerson, however, loved cats with an intensity that created almost unbearable empathy for them. In 1873 the Emersons got two Maltese kittens, whom they named September and Twenty. When four years later Twenty had kittens, daughter Ellen received a note from her mother saying that she "could not come down to dinner, for the cat cried so piteously in the closet that it would be cruel to abuse kitty's confidence in her affection." Once, called by Ellen to see a snowstorm, Lidian declared, "Now here is trouble indeed! The cats will get under the piazza and won't be able to get out, and they will suffer!" (Ellen Tucker Emerson, *Life of Lidian*, xiv–xv). Ellen recalled that September, who lived with the Emersons less than a year, was not deterred by Waldo's aloofness toward pets but was "all the time admiring Father. If Father was in the garden September sat near with lifted head gazing in his face. If he was in the dining-room and September could get in he would immediately assume the same attitude of rapt contemplation" (168). Lidian's affection for pets extended to active commitment to animal rights. An associate member of the Massachusetts Society for the Prevention of Cruelty to Animals (MSPCA) from its founding in 1867, she served as its vice president for Concord in 1872. Ellen remembered distributing copies of the society's monthly magazine, *Our Dumb Animals*, in church pews at her mother's direction. Whether Waldo buckled under spousal pressure or simply had concealed his own feelings under wit and reticence, he too served as a vice president of the MSPCA from 1868 to 1872.

Henry Thoreau also flashed angrily at the cruel treatment of any animal. Edward Waldo Emerson, who as a young boy was befriended by Thoreau, recalled that Thoreau "felt real respect for the personality and character of animals." Later a physician and editor of his father's works, Edward Emerson observed in his older friend the same mutual affection between human and animal companions—the same respect for the integrity and worth of the "lower animals"—that Thoreau professed in his journal: "For all life [Thoreau] had reverence, and just where the limits of conscious life began and ended he was too wise, and too hopeful, to say" (*Henry Thoreau as Remembered*, 82–83). Indeed, several passages in Thoreau's writings express powerful empathy with, and awe toward, the psychic lives of animals, as in this exclamation in his journal for 12 December 1856: "Wonderful, wonderful is our life and that of our companions! That there should be such a thing as a brute animal, not human! and that it should attain to a sort of society with our race!"

Still, on its face, domestic sentiments would seem remote from the world of nature, solitude, and experimentation in *Walden*. Thoreau, in fact, explicitly says that at Walden he "kept neither dog, cat, cow, pig, nor hens, so that you would have said there was a deficiency of domestic sounds; neither the churn, nor the spinning wheel, nor even the singing of the kettle, nor the hissing of the urn, nor children crying, to comfort one. An old-fashioned man would have lost his senses or died of ennui before this" (127). Quite literally, however, *Walden* is a book about housekeeping—from the raising of the house, to furnishing it, to hosting visitors, to gardening, to reflecting and writing about living a life of integrity. Thoreau could have kept domestic animals at Walden only with difficulty, since his two-year, two-month, two-day moratorium to explore transcendental economy was punctuated by a trip to the Maine woods and a night in jail, among other excursions. But the Thoreau household—which Henry never wholly left—was graced by cats, a fact that Ellery Channing emphasized in his attempt to redeem his friend from lingering, posthumous charges that he had been an antisocial hermit: "In his own home he was one of those characters who may be called household treasures . . . fond of the pets, the sister's flowers, or sacred Tabby. Kittens were his favorites,—he would play with them by the half-hour. Some have fancied because he moved to Walden he left his family. He bivouacked there, and really lived at home, where he went every day" (24). As early as 25 April 1841, moreover, Thoreau had asserted the paradox that "[t]here is all of civilized life in the woods—their wildest scenes have an air of domesticity and homeliness" (*Journal* 1:304), and in *Walden* too he called Nature his "home" and described the compatibility between his inner, "domestic" well-being and the external vagaries of weather and the changing seasons (131–32, for example). His extensive, lifelong descriptions, anecdotes, and reflections about dogs and cats are but further evidence that he considered truly domestic qualities to be essentially portable states of mind. The reflections of the "hermit of Walden" on the subjects of home and domestic animals are thus surprisingly consistent with the domestic tradition represented by Mrs. Follen, Miss Alcott, and Mrs. Emerson.

Thoreau's writings about dogs and cats are remarkably diverse and vigorous; indeed, he was provoked by reading Topsell's translation of Gesner to reflect at length in his own journal about the art of "describing an animal." Topsell may have lacked sympathy with cats, but Thoreau praised his capacity to enable the reader "to realize the living creature and its habitat," a capacity missing in much modern scientific writing about animals, which fails to "go beyond the shell." Thoreau declares, "I think that the most important requisite in describing an animal, is to be sure and give its character and spirit.

Introduction

. . . Surely the most important part of an animal is its *anima*, its vital spirit, on which is based its character and all the peculiarities by which it most concerns us. Yet most scientific books which treat of animals leave this out altogether, and what they describe are as it were phenomena of dead matter. . . . If you have undertaken to write the biography of an animal, you will have to present to us the living creature." Whether describing animals or humans, names—the habit of classifying—must not be allowed to smother the sympathetic imagination: "As soon as I begin to be aware of the life of any creature, I at once forget its name. . . . The name is convenient in communicating with others, but it is not to be remembered when I communicate with myself" (*Journal* XIII:149 –55).

Thoreau's descriptions of dogs and cats, ranging from snapshots to substantial narratives, are marked by humor, admiration, pathos, curiosity, annoyance, delight. Just as Marion Schwartz observes that dogs are a "product of culture," so Thoreau remarks in *Walden* that dogs and cats acquire "the same second nature" as humans in becoming domesticated. He is struck by how much companion animals resemble their masters (and how people adapt to their pets), and he finds analogies between domestic and wild animals (foxes/dogs, owls/cats). He quotes—and coins—aphorisms involving dogs and cats. He is fascinated by scientific study of dogs and cats (he investigates the "winged cat") and offers precise observations of behavior; but he is always most concerned "to realize the living creature." He is haunted by the heroic, musical quality of the distant sound of dogs barking in the night and by the unexpected sight of a cat in the woods. Thoreau is no sentimentalist. Concord in his time was an agricultural community, where hunting was ubiquitous and animals were valued for their service. Thus, dogs are sometimes brutal or rabid; they in turn are sometimes lured to destruction by wily foxes. Cats are tormented and drowned. Both dogs and cats on occasion interrupt Thoreau's concentration. But he also fondly describes the exploits of Bose, Ellery Channing's dog, who accompanied the two friends on excursions. It must be admitted that Thoreau is, finally, a "cat person," and his most affectionate descriptions are of plucky kittens and family cats such as Min. No sweeter human portrait exists in Thoreau's writings than a glimpse of his friend the farmer George Minott, who told his wife that he "would not kill a cat for . . . any sum. He thought they loved life as well as we" (19 November 1855).

In the final months of his life, as his energy was being sapped by the symptoms of the tuberculosis that finally killed him, Thoreau curtailed his saunterings and, accordingly, recorded fewer encounters with the hounds whose distant barking he had always found a tonic for the ears. At the same time, confined increasingly to the home, he wrote some of his most extensive and delightful accounts of the kittens in the Thoreau household. Thoreau's late journal records the domestic circle narrowing for a still-young man who had so loved the outdoors; reading it is sad and poignant. Yet, to the end Thoreau is also remarkably brave—and consistent. For kittens are not merely (a favorite Thoreau qualifier) "domestic creatures," and he refuses to succumb to the confines of the house. He loved cats not merely for their beauty, courage, grace, and independence—he remained fascinated by that perennial mystery of felines, who, even as they "incline to affection" with humans, retain the aura of the wild. The Walden experiment had been not a sojourn in the wilderness but an exploration of balance between society and nature reflected in personal integrity. In that oft-misquoted passage, Thoreau did not call for people to move to the wilderness: "Our village life would stagnate if it were not for the unexplored forests and meadows which surround it. We need the tonic of *wildness*" (317; italics added). It had always been an article of faith with him that the domestic and the wild were part of a continuous circle. In "Walking," for example, he is delighted to see even cattle "reassert[ing]" their wildness—"frisking in unwieldy sport . . . even like kittens." The analogy is telling. Thoreau's last extensive journal passages describe little kittens frisking in the home—a more "domestic" image cannot be imagined. But seen from the imagination—and the affections—the cat—that most domestic animal—embodied also the tonic of wildness that for Thoreau was life itself.

🐾   🐾   🐾

Thanks to the humans who have given valuable help and advice in the preparation of this collection: Ron Bosco, past president of the Thoreau Society; Brad Dean, editor of the *Thoreau Society Bulletin*; James S. McDonald, Esq.; Bruce Wilcox, director of the University of Massachusetts Press; Paul M. Wright, sponsoring editor at the press; Carol Betsch, managing editor; and my wife, Sandy, who is responsible for finding most of the dogs and cats who have graced our household.

And fond thanks to the dogs and cats who have shared bonds of affection with me over the years: on the canine side, in memory of Jackie, Nikki, Rhett, Jack Barker, Macaroni, Eleanor, Waldo, Maxie, Sarah, Sheba, Becky, Peter, and Rinny; and on the feline side, to Vincent FinBoy, Buster, Isabel, the elusive Bronson Allcat, Tori, Chloe, Molly, and Abbey, and in memory of Max, Holly, Patty, Cori, Betsy, Bert, Dorian the Hurricat, Thunder, Jean Claude Kitty, Martin, Kim, Socks, and especially Eugene J. McKitty and Jennifur.

Bonds of Affection
Thoreau on Dogs and Cats

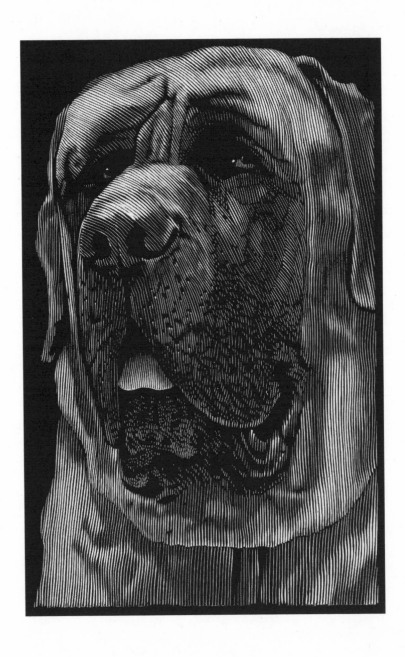

Sept 13th Rowed and sailed to Concord—about 50 miles."

I shall not soon forget my first night in a tent—how the distant barking of dogs for so many still hours revealed to me the riches of the night.— Who would not be a dog and bay the moon? —

13 September 1839, Journal *1:137*

With noble perseverance the dog bays the stars yonder — — I too like thee walk alone in this strange familiar night— My voice like thine beating against its friendly concave, and barking I hear only my own voice. 10. o'clock.

24 June 1840, Journal *1:142*

We are as much refreshed by sounds, as by sights—or scents—or flavors—as the barking of a dog heard in the woods at midnight, or the tinklings which attend the dawn.

As I picked blackberries this morning by starlight, the distant yelping of a dog fell on my inward ear, as the cool breeze on my cheek.

16 July 1840, Journal *1:158*

The very dogs that sullenly bay the moon from farm yards o' these nights, evince more heroism than is tamely barked forth in all the civil exhortations and war sermons of the age.

31 July 1840, Journal *1:164*

IT IS A RARE soundness when cow-bells and horns are heard from over the fields— And now I see the beauty and full meaning of that word sound. Nature always possesses a certain sonorousness, as in the hum of insects—the booming of ice—the crowing of cocks in the morning and the barking of dogs in the night—which indicates her sound state. God's voice is but a clear bell sound. I drink in a wonderful health—a cordial—in sound. The effect of the slightest tinkling in the horizon measures my own soundness.

3 March 1841, Journal *1:277*

THE MAN OF GENIUS, like a dog with a bone, or the slave who has swallowed a diamond, or a patient with the gravel, sits afar and retired, off the road, hangs out no sign of refreshment for man and beast, but says, by all possible hints and signs, I wish to be alone,—good-by,—farewell. But the Landlord can afford to live without privacy.

"The Landlord," Excursions and Poems, *157*

WE SAW LAST SUMMER, on the side of a mountain, a dog employed to churn for a farmer's family, travelling upon a horizontal wheel, and though he had sore eyes, an alarming cough, and withal a demure aspect, yet their bread did get buttered for all that. Undoubtedly, in the most brilliant successes, the first rank is always sacrificed.

"Paradise (To Be) Regained," Reform Papers, *23*

HAVE YOU SEEN my hound sir— I want to know What— Lawyer's office—law Books if you've seen anything of a hound about here— why, what do you do here? I live here. no I have'nt haven't you heard one In the woods anyplace O yes I heard one this morning— What do you do here— but he was someway off— Which side did he seem to be— Well I should think here this other side of the pond.— This is a large dog makes a large track—he's been out hunting from Lexington for a week. How long have you lived here— Oh about a year Some body said there was a man up here had a camp in the woods somewhere and he'd got him Well I dont know of any body— There's Brittons camp over on the other road— It may be there—

After 23 December 1845, Journal *2:190*

LATE IN THE AFTERNOON we passed a man on the shore fishing with a long birch pole, its silvery bark left on, and a dog at his side, rowing so near as to agitate his cork with our oars, and drive away luck for a season; and when we had rowed a mile as straight as an arrow, with our faces turned towards him, and the bubbles in our wake still visible on the tranquil surface, there stood the fisher still with his dog, like statues under the other side of the heavens, the only objects to relieve the eye in the extended meadow; and there would he stand abiding his luck, till he took his way home through the fields at evening with his fish. Thus, by one bait or another, Nature allures inhabitants into all her recesses. This man was the last of our townsmen whom we saw, and we silently through him bade adieu to our friends.

"Saturday," A Week on the Concord and Merrimack Rivers, *23*

[T]HE MOST CONSTANT and memorable sound of a summer's night, which we did not fail to hear every night afterward, though at no time so incessantly and so favorably as now, was the barking of the house dogs, from the loudest and hoarsest bark to the faintest aerial palpitation under the eaves of heaven, from the patient but anxious mastiff to the timid and wakeful terrier, at first loud and rapid, then faint and slow, to be imitated only in a whisper; wow-wow-wow-wow—wo——wo——w——w. Even in a retired and uninhabited district like this, it was a sufficiency of sound for the ear of night, and more impressive than any music. I have heard the voice of a hound, just before daylight, while the stars were shining, from over the woods and river, far in the horizon, when it sounded as sweet and melodious as an instrument. The hounding of a dog pursuing a fox or other animal in the horizon, may have first suggested the notes of the hunting horn to alternate with and relieve the lungs of the dog. This natural bugle long resounded in the woods of the ancient world before the horn was invented. The very dogs that sullenly bay the moon from farm-yards in these nights, excite more heroism in our breasts than all the civil exhortations or war sermons of the age. "I had rather be a dog, and bay the moon," than many a Roman that I know.

"Saturday," A Week on the Concord and Merrimack Rivers, *41* (see also 1842–1844, Journal *2:14–15*)

THERE WAS a Concord man once who had a fox hound named Burgoyne—he called him Bugīne. A good name

30 May 1851, Journal *3:241*

RIDING TO SURVEY a woodlot yesterday I observed that a dog accompanied the wagon— Having tied the horse at the last house and entered the woods, I saw no more of the dog while there;—but when riding back to the village I saw the dog again running by the wagon—and in answer to my inquiry was told that the horse & wagon were hired & that the dog always accompanied the horse. I queried whether it might happen that a dog would accompany the wagon if a strange horse were put into it—whether he would ever attach himself to an inanimate object. Methinks the driver though a stranger as it were added intellect to the mere animality of the horse and the dog not making very nice distinctions yielded respect to the horse and equipage as if it were human If the horse were to trot off alone without wagon or driver—I think it doubtful if the dog would follow—if with the wagon then the chances of his following would be increased—but if with a driver though a stranger I have found by experience that he would follow.

29 June 1851, Journal *3:279–80*

THE WIND now rising from over Bear Garden Hill falls gently on my ear & delivers its message the same that I have heard passing over bare & stoney *mt* tops — So uncontaminated & untamed is the wind. The air that has swept over caucasus & the sands of Arabia comes to breathe on New England fields. The dogs bark they are not as much stiller as man. They are on the alert suspecting the approach of foes. The darkness perchance affects them—makes them mad & wild—

5 August 1851, Journal *3:353*

SOME DOGS I have noticed have a propensity to worry cows— they go off by themselves to distant pastures & ever and anon like four legged devils they worry the cows—full of the devil. They are so full of the devil they know not what to do. I come to interfere between the cows & their tormentors. Ah I grieve to see the devils escape so easily by their swift limbs imps of mischief— They are the dog state of those boys who pull down hand bills in the streets. Their next migration perchance will be into such dogs as these—ignoble fate. The dog whose office it should be to guard the herd turned its tormentor. Some courageous cow endeavoring in vain to toss the nimble devil.

18 August 1851, Journal *3:373*

JOHN HOSMER'S dog sprang up, ran out, & growled at us—and in his eye I seemed to see the eye of his master. I have no doubt but that as is the master such in course of time tend to become his herds & flocks as well as dogs—

4 September 1851, Journal *4:37–38*

SAW WHAT I THOUGHT a small red dog in the road—which cantered along over the bridge this side the Powder mills—& then turned into the woods. This decided me—this turning into the woods—that it was a fox. The dog of the woods The dog that is more at home in the woods than in the roads & fields. I do not often see a dog turning into the woods.

4 September 1851, Journal *4:45*

ABOUT VILLAGES You hear the bark of dogs instead of the howl of wolves—

5 October 1851, Journal *4:121*

THE SOUND OF FOX-HOUNDS in the woods heard now at 9 Am in the village—reminds me of mild winter mornings.

9 October 1851, Journal *4:134*

8½ AM UP THE RIVER in a boat to Pelham's Pond with W.E[llery] C[hanning]
 . . . Observed the verification of the scripture saying "as the dog returns to his vomit?"? Our black pup sole passenger in the stern, perhaps made sea-sick—vomited then cleaned the boat again most faithfully—and with a bright eye—licking his chops & looking round for more.

15 October 1851, Journal *4:147, 149*

I AWOKE this morning to infinite regret. In my dream. . . .
Again I was in my own small pleasure boat—learning to sail on
the sea—& I raised my sail before my anchor which I dragged
far into the sea— I saw the buttons which had come off the coats
of drowned men—and suddenly I saw my dog—when I knew
not that I had one—standing in the sea up to his chin to warm
his legs which had been wet—which the cool wind numbed.

26 October 1851, Journal *4:154*

THE SNOW has been for some time more than a foot deep on a
level, and some roads drifted quite full. . . . The snow melts on
the surface. The warmth of the sun reminds me of summer—
The dog runs before us on the R R cause way & appears to
enjoy it as much as ourselves. C. remarks truly that most people
do not distinguish between a pup & a dog—& treat both alike
though the former may not yet have a tooth in his head. . . .
Ah then the brook beyond—its rippling waters & its sunny
sands.— . . . The sun reflected from the sandy gravelly bottom
. . . enabled me to realize summer. But the dog partly spoiled the
transparency of the water by running in the brook. A pup that
had never seen a summer brook.

25 January 1852, Journal *4:284, 286*

DAY BEFORE YESTERDAY I saw the hunters out with a dozen
dogs—but only 2 pussies one white & one little gray one did I
see—for so many men & dogs who seem to set all the village
a-stir, as if the fox's trail led through it.

29 January 1852, Journal *4:303*

WHEN THE THERMOMETER is down to 20° in the morning, as last month, I think of the poor dogs who have no masters.

If a poor dog has no master, every body will throw a billet of wood at him. it never rains but it pours

11 February 1852, Journal *4:341*

THE EMPRESSEMENT of a little dog when he starts any wild thing in the woods! The woods ring with his barking as if the tragedy of Actaeon were being acted over again.

24 February 1852, Journal *4:364*

BEFORE SUNRISE

With what infinite & unwearied expectation and proclamations the cocks usher in every dawn as if there had never been one before. & the dogs bark still—& the thallus of lichens springs— So tenacious of life is nature.

16 March 1852, Journal *4:391*

DOGS BAYING THE MOON.

Says of the Canis Familiaris variety Canadensis (North American Dog) by which he means that "most generally cultivated by the native tribes of Canada, and the Hudson's Bay countries"—"All the dogs of a camp assemble at night to howl in unison, particularly when the moon shines bright."

Transcribed from Sir John Richardson, Fauna Boreali-Americana *(1829–1837)*, Thoreau's Fact Book, *1:87–88*

Thoreau on Dogs

I HAVE SINCE LEARNED that the English traveler Warburton remarked, soon after landing at Quebec, that everything was cheap there but men. That must be the difference between going thither from New and from Old England. I had already observed the dogs harnessed to their little milk-carts, which contain a single large can, lying asleep in the gutters regardless of the horses, while they rested from their labors, at different stages of the ascent in the Upper Town. I was surprised at the regular and extensive use made of these animals for drawing not only milk but groceries, wood, etc. It reminded me that the dog commonly is not put to any use. Cats catch mice; but dogs only worry the cats. Kalm, a hundred years ago, saw sledges here for ladies to ride in, drawn by a pair of dogs. He says, "A middle-sized dog is sufficient to draw a single person, when the roads are good;" and he was told by old people that horses were very scarce in their youth, and almost all the land-carriage was then effected by dogs. They made me think of the Esquimaux, who, in fact, are the next people on the north. Charlevoix says that the first horses were introduced in 1665.

"Quebec and Montmorenci," A Yankee in Canada, *in* Excursions and Poems, *30*

THE ROAD in this clayey-looking soil was exceedingly muddy in consequence of the night's rain. We met an old woman directing her dog, which was harnessed to a little cart, to the least muddy part of it. It was a beggarly sight. But harnessed to the cart as he was, we heard him barking after we had passed, though we looked anywhere but to the cart to see where the dog was that barked.

"St. Anne," A Yankee in Canada, *in* Excursions and Poems, *44*

Bonds of Affection

WHEN WE REACHED the bridge between St. Anne and Château Richer, I ran back a little way to ask a man in the field the name of the river which we were crossing, but for a long time I could not make out what he said, for he was one of the more unintelligible Jacques Cartier men. At last it flashed upon me that it was *La Rivière au Chien*, or the Dog River, which my eyes beheld, which brought to my mind the life of the Canadian voyageur and *coureur de bois*, a more western and wilder Arcadia, methinks, than the world has ever seen; for the Greeks, with all their wood and river gods, were not so qualified to name the natural features of a country as the ancestors of these French Canadians; and if any people had a right to substitute their own for the Indian names, it was they. They have preceded the pioneer on our own frontiers, and named the *prairie* for us. *La Rivière au Chien* cannot, by any license of language, be translated into Dog River, for that is not such a giving it to the dogs, and recognizing their place in creation, as the French implies. One of the tributaries of the St. Anne is named *La Rivière de la Rose;* and farther east are *La Rivière de la Blondelle* and *La Rivière de la Friponne.* Their very *rivière* meanders more than our *river.*

"*St. Anne,*" A Yankee in Canada, *in* Excursions and Poems, *56*

ISRAEL RICES dog stood stock still so long that I took him at a distance for the end of a bench. He looked much like a fox—& his fur was as soft. . . . It seems to be a part of the economy of nature to make dogs make water against upright objects that so her plants may get watered & manurred. It is a part of her husbandry.

. . . On the rocky point of this island where the wind is felt the waves are breaking merrily—and now for half an hour our dog has been standing in the water & ceaselessly snapping at each wave as it broke as if it were a living creature. He regardless of cold & wet thrusts his head into each wave to gripe it. A dog snapping at the waves as they break on a rocky shore. He then rolls himself in the leaves for a napkin.

2 April 1852, Journal *4:417, 418, 420*

THAT IS A pleasant part of the north river under the black-birches. The dog does not hesitate to take to the water for a stick but the current carries him rapidly down.

12 April 1852, Journal *4:439*

V THAT SENTENCE in Gilpin about—A gentleman might keep a greyhound within ten miles of the forest if he was *lawed*— "*Lawing,* or *expeditation,* was a forest-term for disqualifying a dog to exert such speed, as was necessary to take a deer. It was performed either by cutting out the sole of his foot, or by taking off two of his claws by a chisel, and mallet."

It reminds me of the majority of human hounds that tread the forests paths of this world—they go slightly limping in their gait as if disqualified by a cruel fate to overtake the nobler game of the forest—their natural quarry— Most men are such dogs. Ever & anon starting a quarry—with perfect scent which from this cruel maiming & disqualification of the fates he is incapable of coming up with. Does not the noble dog shed tears?

15 April 1852, Journal *4:451–52*

2 Pm to River

A driving rain i.e. a rain with Easterly wind & driving mists.
. . . Going through Dennis' field with C. saw a flock of geese
on E. side of river near willows. 12 great birds on the troubled
surface of the meadow delayed by the storm. . . . We remained
close under our umbrella by the tree—ever and anon looking
through a peep hole between the umbrella & the tree at the
birds—on they came, sometimes in 2 sometimes in 3 squads—
warily—till we could see the steel blue & green reflections from
their necks. We held the dog close the while C lying on his back
in the rain had him in his arms—and thus we gradually edged
round on the ground in this cold wet windy storm keeping our
feet to the tree & the great calf of a dog with his eyes shut in our
arms. We laughed well at our adventure.

18 April 1852, Journal *4:465*

A strange dog accompanied us today—a hunting dog—
gyrating about us at a great distance—beating every bush &
barking at the birds. with great spead—gyrating his tail too
all the while. I thought of what Gilpin says, that he sailed &
steered by means of his tail— . . . . Our dog sends off a partridge
with a whir far across the open field & the river like a winged
bullet— . . . .

. . . This strange dog has good habits for a companion he
keeps so distant— He never trusts himself near us though he
accompanies us for miles.

22 April 1852, Journal *4:483–84*

PRAY LET US LIVE without being drawn by dogs—esquimaux fashion—a scrambling pack tearing over hill & vale—& biting each others ears. What a despicable mode of progressing to be drawn by a pack of dogs'— Why not by a flock of mice?

5 June 1852, Journal *5:80*

BOYS ARE BATHING at Hubbards Bend playing with a boat. (I at the willows) The color of their bodies in the sun at a distance is pleasing—the not often seen flesh color— . . . As yet we have not man in nature. What a singular fact for an angel visitant to this earth to carry back in his note book that men were forbidden to expose their bodies under the severest penalties.— A pale pink which the sun would soon tan. White men! There are no white men to contrast with the red & the black—they are of such colors as the weaver gives them. I wonder that the dog knows his master when he goes in to bathe & does not stay by his clothes.

11 June 1852, Journal *5:90–91*

I OBSERVED A BULLOCK this afternoon when all his companions on a side hill were already looking at me—suddenly whirl round to stare as if he had detected from their attitudes that some object engaged them. Then how curiously a whole herd will leave off grazing & stare till you have passed.— & if you have a dog—will think of their calves and make demonstration of tossing him.

23 June 1852, Journal *5:130*

COME TO EAT the grass? It is the biggest game our dog starts. Much of the June grass is dead. *Most* of it in Dry fields. . . . The dog worried a wood chuck half grown—which did not turn its back & run into its hole but backed into it & faced him & us gritting its teeth & prepared to die. But even this little fellow was able to defend himself against the dog with his sharp teeth. That fierce gritting of their teeth is a remarkable habit with these animals.

24 June 1852, Journal *5:143*

HOW WELL BEHAVED are cows!— When they approach me reclining in the shade—from curiosity—or to receive a whisp of grass or to share the shade—or to lick the dog held up—like a calf—though just now they ran at him to toss him—they do not obtrude

1 July 1852, Journal *5:166*

C[HANNING] says he keeps a dog for society—to stir up the air of the room when it becomes dead—for he experiences awful solitudes.— Another time thinks we must cultivate the social qualities—perhaps had better keep 2 dogs apiece.

11 August 1852, Journal *5:293*

Richard Harlan M. D. in his Fauna Americana 1825 says of man that those parts are "most hairy, which in animals are most bare, viz. the axillae and pubes."

. . .

Harlan says that when white is associated with another color on a dog's tail it is always terminal—& that the observations of Desmarest confirm it.

26 October 1852, Journal *5:386*

At Cambridge today. Dr Harris thinks the Indians had no real hemp but their apocynum—and he thinks a kind of nettle—& an asclepias. &c. He doubts if the dog was indigenous among them— Finds nothing to convince him in the history of N. England. Agassiz asked him what authority there was for it

9 February 1853, Journal *5:464*

To day the weather is severely and remarkably cold—...
... In the woods beyond Peter's we heard our dog, a large Newfoundland dog—barking at something—& going forward were amused to see him barking while he retreated with fear at that black oak with remarkable excrescence—which had been cut off just above it—leaving it like some misshapen idol about the height of a man. Though we set him onto it—he did not venture within 3 or four rods. I would not have believed that he would notice any such strange thing.

15 March 1853, Journal *6:10*

WE SAILED all the way back from the Baker Farm though the wind blew very nearly at right angles with the river much of the way—. . . . The dog swam for long distances behind us. . . . We taste at each cool spring with which we are acquainted in the bank—making haste to reach it before the dog—who otherwise is sure to be found cooling himself in it. We some times use him on board to sit in in the stern & trim the boat while we both row—for he is heavy and other wise we sink the bows to much in the water—but he has a habit of standing too near the rower—& each time recieving a fillip under the chin from the rowers fists— So at last he tumbles himself overboard & takes a riparial excursion— And we are amused to see how judicicously he selects his points for crossing the river from time to time in order to avoid long circuits made by bays & meadows & keep as near us as possible.

16 June 1853, Journal *6:210–11*

THE DISTANT VILLAGE sounds, are the barking of dogs, that animal with which man has allied himself, and the rattling of wagons— For the farmers have gone into to town ashopping this Saturday night— The dog is the tamed wolf—as the villager is the tamed savage

18 June 1853, Journal *6:223-24*

Thoreau on Dogs

On Saturday, the 26th, a dog on whose collar the words "Milton Hill," or equivalent ones, were engraved ran through the town, having, as the story went, bitten a boy in Lincoln. He bit several dogs in this town and was finally shot. Some of the dogs bitten have been killed, and rumor now says that the boy died yesterday. People are considerably alarmed. Some years ago a boy in Lincoln was bitten by a raccoon and died of hydrophobia. I observed to Minott to-night that I did not think that our doctors knew how to cure this disease, but he said they could cure it, he had seen a man bitten who was cured. The story is worth telling, for it shows how much trouble the passage of one mad dog through the town may produce.

It was when he was a boy and lived down below the old Ben Prescott house, over the cellar-hole on what is now Hawthorne's land. The first he remembers a couple of men had got poles and were punching at a strange dog toward night under a barn in that neighborhood. The dog, which was speckled and not very large, would growl and bite the pole, and they ran a good deal of risk, but they did not know that he was mad. At length they routed him, and he took to the road and came on towards town, and Minott, keeping his distance, followed on behind. When the dog got to the old Ben Prescott place, he turned up into the yard, where there were a couple of turkeys, drove them into a corner, bit off the head of one, and carried the body off across the road into the meadow opposite. They then raised the cry of "Mad dog." He saw his mother and Aunt Prescott, two old ladies, coming down the road, while the dog was running the other way in the meadow, and he shouted to them to take care of themselves, for that dog was mad. The dog soon reëntered the road at some bars and held on toward town. Minott next saw Harry Hooper coming down the road after his cows, and he shouted to him to look out, for the dog was mad, but Harry, who was in the middle of the road, spread his arms out, one on each side, and, being short, the dog leaped right upon his open breast and made a pass at his throat, but missed it, though it frightened him a good deal; and Minott, coming up, exclaimed, "Why, you're crazy, Harry; if he 'd 'a' bitten ye, 't would 'a' killed ye." When he got up as far as the red house or Curtis place, the dog was about in the middle of the road, and a large and stout old gentleman by the name of Fay, dressed in small-clothes, was coming down on the sidewalk. M. shouted to him also to take care of himself, for the dog was mad, and Fay said afterward that he heard him but he had always supposed that a mad dog would n't turn out for anything; but when this dog was nearly abreast of him, he suddenly inclined toward him, and then again inclined still more, and seized him by the left leg just below the knee, and Fay, giving him a kick with the other leg, tripped himself up; and when he was down, the dog bit him in the right leg in the same place. Being by this time well frightened, and fearing that he would spring at his throat next, Fay seized the dog himself by his throat and held him fast, and called lustily for somebody to come and kill him. A man by the name of Lewis rushed out of the red house with an old axe and began to tap on the dog's nose with it, but he was afraid to strike harder, for Fay told him not to hit him. Minott saw it all, but still kept his distance. Suddenly Fay, not knowing what he did, let go, and the man, giving the dog a blow across the back, ran into the house; but, it being a dull meat axe, the dog trotted along, still toward town.

He turned and went round the pond by Bowers's and, going down to the brook by the roadside, lapped some water. Just then, Peter coming over the bridge, the dog reared up and growled at him, and he, seeing that he was mad, made haste through the bars out of his way and cut across the fields to Reuben Brown's. The dog went on, it being now between sundown and dark, to Peter Wheeler's, and bit two cows, which afterward died of hydrophobia, and next he went to where Nathan Stow now lives, and bit a goose in the wing, and so he kept on through the town. The next that was heard of him, Black Cato, that lived at the Lee place, now Sam Wheeler's, on the river, was waked up about midnight by a noise among the pigs, and, having got up, he took a club and went out to see what was the matter. Looking over into the pen, this dog reared up at him, and he knocked him back into it, and, jumping over, mauled him till he thought he was dead and then tossed him out. In the morning he thought he [would] go out and see whose dog he had killed, but lo! he had picked himself up, and there was no dog to be found.

Cato was going out into the woods chopping that day, and as he was getting over a wall lined with brush, the same dog reared up at him once more, but this time, having heard of the mad dog, he was frightened and ran; but still the dog came on, and once or twice he knocked him aside with a large stone, till at length, the dog coming close to him, he gave him a blow which killed him; and lest he should run away again, he cut off his head and threw both head and body into the river.

In the meanwhile Fay went home (to the Dr. Heywood house), drank some spirit, then went straight over to Dr. Heywood's office and stayed there and was doctored by him for three weeks. The doctor cut out the mangled flesh and made various applications, and Fay cried like a baby, but he never experienced any further ill effects from the bite.

29 November 1853, Journal *V:522–25*

Bonds of Affection

I LONG AGO LOST a hound, a bay horse, and a turtle-dove, and am still on their trail. Many are the travellers I have spoken concerning them, describing their tracks and what calls they answered to. I have met one or two who had heard the hound, and the tramp of the horse, and even seen the dove disappear behind a cloud, and they seemed as anxious to recover them as if they had lost them themselves.

"Economy," Walden, *17*

LATE IN THE EVENING I heard the distant rumbling of wagons over bridges,—a sound heard farther than almost any other at night,—the baying of dogs, and sometimes again the lowing of some disconsolate cow in a distant barn-yard.

"Sounds," Walden, *126*

ONCE OR TWICE . . . while I lived at the pond, I found myself ranging the woods, like a half-starved hound, with a strange abandonment, seeking some kind of venison which I might devour, and no morsel could have been too savage for me.

"Higher Laws," Walden, *210*

Hermit. I WONDER what the world is doing now. I have not heard so much as a locust over the sweet-fern these three hours. . . . Who would live there where a body can never think for the barking of Bose? . . . Hark! I hear a rustling of the leaves. Is it some ill-fed village hound yielding to the instinct of the chase? or the lost pig which is said to be in these woods, whose tracks I saw after the rain? It comes on apace; my sumachs and sweet-briars tremble.—Eh, Mr. Poet, is it you? How do you like the world to-day?

"Brute Neighbors," Walden, *223*

MANY A VILLAGE BOSE, fit only to course a mud-turtle in a victualling cellar, sported his heavy quarters in the woods, without the knowledge of his master, and ineffectually smelled at old fox burrows and woodchucks' holes; led perchance by some slight cur which nimbly threaded the wood, and might still inspire a natural terror in its denizens;—now far behind his guide, barking like a canine bull toward some small squirrel which had treed itself for scrutiny, then, cantering off, bending the bushes with his weight, imagining that he is on the track of some stray member of the gerbille family.

"Brute Neighbors," Walden, *232*

SOMETIMES I HEARD the foxes as they ranged over the snow crust, in moonlight nights, in search of a partridge or other game, barking raggedly and demoniacally like forest dogs, as if laboring with some anxiety, or seeking expression, struggling for light and to be dogs outright and run freely in the streets; for if we take the ages into our account, may there not be a civilization going on among brutes as well as men? They seemed to me to be rudimental, burrowing men, still standing on their defence, awaiting their transformation. Sometimes one came near to my window, attracted by my light, barked a vulpine curse at me, and then retreated.

"Winter Animals," Walden, *273*

IN DARK WINTER MORNINGS, or in short winter afternoons, I sometimes heard a pack of hounds threading all the woods with hounding cry and yelp, unable to resist the instinct of the chase, and the note of the hunting horn at intervals, proving that man was in the rear. . . . They tell me that if the fox would remain in the bosom of the frozen earth he would be safe, or if he would

run in a straight line away no fox-hound could overtake him.
. . . A hunter told me that he once saw a fox pursued by hounds
burst out on to Walden when the ice was covered with shal-
low puddles, run part way across, and then return to the same
shore. Ere long the hounds arrived, but here they lost the scent.
Sometimes a pack hunting by themselves would pass my door,
and circle round my house, and yelp and hound without regard-
ing me, as if afflicted by a species of madness, so that nothing
could divert them from the pursuit. Thus they circle until they
fall upon the recent trail of a fox, for a wise hound will forsake
every thing else for this. One day a man came to my hut from
Lexington to inquire after his hound that made a large track,
and had been hunting for a week by himself. But I fear that he
was not the wiser for all I told him, for every time I attempted
to answer his questions he interrupted me by asking, "What do
you do here?" He had lost a dog, but found a man.

One old hunter who has a dry tongue, who used to come to
bathe in Walden once every year when the water was warmest,
and at such times looked in upon me, told me, that many years
ago he took his gun one afternoon and went out for a cruise in
Walden Wood; and as he walked the Wayland road he heard
the cry of hounds approaching, and ere long a fox leaped the
wall into the road, and as quick as thought leaped the other
wall out of the road, and his swift bullet had not touched him.
Some way behind came an old hound and her three pups in
full pursuit, hunting on their own account, and disappeared
again in the woods. Late in the afternoon, as he was resting
in the thick woods south of Walden, he heard the voice of the
hounds far over toward Fair Haven still pursuing the fox; and
on they came, their hounding cry which made all the woods
ring sounding nearer and nearer, now from Well-Meadow, now
from the Baker Farm. For a long time he stood still and listened
to their music, so sweet to a hunter's ear, when suddenly the

fox appeared, threading the solemn aisles with an easy cours-
ing pace, whose sound was concealed by a sympathetic rustle
of the leaves, swift and still, keeping the ground, leaving his
pursuers far behind; and, leaping upon a rock amid the woods,
he sat erect and listening, with his back to the hunter. For a
moment compassion restrained the latter's arm; but that was a
short-lived mood, and as quick as thought can follow thought
his piece was levelled, and *whang!*—the fox rolling over the
rock lay dead on the ground. The hunter still kept his place
and listened to the hounds. Still on they came, and now the
near woods resounded through all their aisles with their demo-
niac cry. At length the old hound burst into view with muzzle
to the ground, and snapping the air as if possessed, and ran
directly to the rock; but spying the dead fox she suddenly
ceased her hounding, as if struck dumb with amazement, and
walked round and round him in silence; and one by one her
pups arrived, and, like their mother, were sobered into silence
by the mystery. Then the hunter came forward and stood in
their midst, and the mystery was solved. They waited in silence
while he skinned the fox, then followed the brush a while, and at
length turned off into the woods again. That evening a Weston
Squire came to the Concord hunter's cottage to inquire for his
hounds, and told how for a week they had been hunting on their
own account from Weston woods. The Concord hunter told him
what he knew and offered him the skin; but the other declined
it and departed. He did not find his hounds that night, but the
next day learned that they had crossed the river and put up at
a farm-house for the night, whence, having been well fed, they
took their departure early in the morning.

The hunter who told me this could remember one Sam
Nutting, who used to hunt bears on Fair Haven Ledges, and
exchange their skins for rum in Concord village; who told him,
even, that he had seen a moose there. Nutting had a famous fox-

hound named Burgoyne,—he pronounced it Bugine,—which my informant used to borrow. . . .

At midnight, when there was a moon, I sometimes met with hounds in my path prowling about the woods, which would skulk out of my way, as if afraid, and stand silent amid the bushes till I had passed.

"Winter Animals," Walden, *276–80*

SOME ARE dinning in our ears that we Americans, and moderns generally, are intellectual dwarfs compared with the ancients, or even the Elizabethan men. But what is that to the purpose? A living dog is better than a dead lion. Shall a man go and hang himself because he belongs to the race of pygmies, and not be the biggest pygmy that he can? Let every one mind his own business, and endeavor to be what he was made.

"Conclusion," Walden, *325–26*

NIGHT IS THE TIME to hear; our senses took in every sound from the meadows and the village. At first we were disturbed by the screeching of the locomotive and rumbling of the cars, but soon were left to the fainter natural sounds,—the creaking of the crickets, . . . the occasional faint lowing of a cow and the distant barking of dogs, as in a whisper. Our ears drank in every sound. . . . A slight zephyr wafted us almost imperceptibly into the middle of Fair Haven Pond, while we lay watching and listening. . . . [W]e heard the distant sound of the wind through the pines on the hilltop. Or, if we listened closely, we heard still the faint and distant barking of dogs. They rule the night.

7 September 1854, Journal *VII:21–23.*

I AM SURPRISED to find how fast the dog can run in a straight
line on the ice. I am not sure that I can beat him on skates, but
I can turn much shorter.

20 December 1854, Journal *VII:88*

[AT AN INDIAN VILLAGE near Lincoln, Maine] As we walked
up to the nearest house, we were met by a sally of a dozen wolf-
ish-looking dogs, which may have been lineal descendants from
the ancient Indian dogs, which the first voyageurs describe
as "their wolves." I suppose they were. The occupant soon
appeared, with a long pole in his hand, with which he beat off
the dogs, while he parleyed with us.

"Ktaadn," The Maine Woods, *9*

THE CHICKENS HERE were protected by the dogs. As McCauslin
said, "The old one took it up first, and she taught the pup, and
now they had got it into their heads that it wouldn't do to have
anything of the bird kind on the premises." A hawk hovering
over was not allowed to alight, but barked off by the dogs cir-
cling underneath; and a pigeon, or a "yellow hammer," as they
called the pigeon-woodpecker, on a dead limb or stump, was
instantly expelled. It was the main business of their day, and
kept them constantly coming and going. One would rush out of
the house on the least alarm given by the other.

"Ktaadn," The Maine Woods, *25 (see also Fall 1846, Journal 2:301)*

THERE WAS the usual long-handled axe of the primitive woods
by the door . . . and a large, shaggy dog, whose nose, report said,
was full of porcupine quills. I can testify that he looked very
sober. This is the usual fortune of pioneer dogs, for they have
to face the brunt of the battle for their race, and act the part of

Arnold Winkelried without intending it. If he should invite one of his town friends up this way, suggesting moose-meat and unlimited freedom, the latter might pertinently inquire, "What is that sticking in your nose?" When a generation or two have used up all the enemies' darts, their successors lead a comparatively easy life. We owe to our fathers analogous blessings. Many old people receive pensions for no other reason, it seems to me, but as a compensation for having lived a long time ago. No doubt, our town dogs still talk, in a snuffling way, about the days that tried dogs' noses.

"Chesuncook," The Maine Woods, *127*

ANOTHER INDIAN SAID, that the moose, once scared, would run all day. A dog will hang to their lips, and be carried along till he is swung against a tree and drops off.

"Chesuncook," The Maine Woods, *138*
(see also 26 November 1850, Journal *3:153)*

I ASKED NEPTUNE if they had any of the old breed of dogs yet. He answered, "Yes." "But that," said I, pointing to one that had just come in, "is a Yankee dog." He assented. I said that he did not look like a good one. "Oh, yes!" he said, and he told, with much gusto, how, the year before, he had caught and held by the throat a wolf. A very small black puppy rushed into the room and made at the Governor's feet, as he sat in his stockings with his legs dangling from the bedside. The Governor rubbed his hands and dared him to come on, entering into the sport with spirit. Nothing more that was significant transpired, to my knowledge, during this interview. This was the first time that I ever called on a governor, but, as I did not ask for an office, I can speak of it with the more freedom.

"Chesuncook," The Maine Woods, *149*

AT THE BANGOR HOUSE we took in 4 men bound on a hunting excursion, one of the men going as cook. They had a dog, a middling sized brindled cur which ran by the side of the stage, his master showing his head and whistling from time to time; but after we had gone about 3 miles, the dog was suddenly missing, and two of the party went back for him while the stage, which was full of passengers, waited. I suggested that he had taken the back track for the Bangor House. At length one man came back, while the other kept on. This whole party of hunters declared their intention to stop till the dog was found, but the very obliging driver was ready to wait a spell longer. He was evidently unwilling to lose so many passengers, who would have taken a private conveyance, or perhaps the other line of stages the next day. Such progress did we make, with a journey of over 60 miles to be accomplished that day, and a rainstorm just setting in. We discussed the subject of dogs and their instincts till it was threadbare, while we waited there, and the scenery of the suburbs of Bangor is still distinctly impressed on my memory. After full half an hour the man returned, leading the dog by a rope. He had overtaken him just as he was entering the Bangor House. He was then tied on the top of the stage, but being wet and cold, several times in the course of the journey he jumped off, and I saw him dangling by his neck. This dog was depended on to stop bears with. He had already stopped one somewhere in New Hampshire, and I can testify that he stopped a stage in Maine. This party of four probably paid nothing for the dog's ride, nor for his run, while our party of three paid nine dollars, and were charged four for the light canoe which lay still on the top.

"*The Allegash and East Branch,*" The Maine Woods, *159–60*

VERY MUSICAL and even sweet now, like a horn, is the hounding of a foxhound heard now in some distant wood, while I stand listening in some far solitary and silent field.

20 January 1855, Journal *VII:128*

MINOTT. . . . [t]old how Jake Lakin lost a dog, a very valuable one, by a fox leading him on to the ice on the Great Meadows and drowning him.

30 January 1855, Journal *VII:154*

LAST YEAR [Humphrey Buttrick's] dog caught seven black ducks so far grown that he got sixty cents a pair for them; takes a pretty active dog to catch such. . . . He shot a white-headed eagle from Carlisle Bridge. It fell in the water, and his dog was glad to let it alone.

3 May 1855, Journal *VII:353–54*

IT IS REMARKABLE how much the river has been tracked by dogs the week past, not accompanied by their masters. They hunt, perchance, in the night more than is supposed, for I very rarely see one alone by day.

24 January 1856, Journal *VIII:138*

P.M.—UP RIVER IN BOAT.
. . . Melvin floats slowly and quietly along the willows, watching for rats resting there, his white hound sitting still and grave in the prow, and every little while we hear his gun announcing the death of a rat or two. The dog looks on understandingly and makes no motion.

7 April 1856, Journal *VIII: 256–57*

I GO ACROSS LOTS like a hunting dog. With what tireless energy and abandonment they dash through the brush and up the sides of hills! I meet two white foxhounds, led by an old red one. How full of it they are! How their tails work! They are not tied to paths; they burst forth from the thickest shrub oak lot, and immediately dive into another as the fox did.

10 August 1856, Journal *VIII:460*

I AM AMUSED to see four little Irish boys only five or six years old getting a horse in a pasture. . . . At length, by dint of pulling and shouting, they get him into a run down a hill. . . . They haul up at last at the bars, which are down, and then the family puppy, a brown pointer (?), about two-thirds grown, comes bounding to join them and assist. He is as youthful and about as knowing as any of them. The horse marches gravely behind. . . .

2 October 1856, Journal *IX:98*

YESTERDAY MORNING I noticed that several people were having their pigs killed, not foreseeing the thaw. . . .

I saw Lynch's dog stealthily feeding at a half of his master's pig, which lay dressed on a wheelbarrow at the door. A little yellow-brown dog, with fore feet braced on the ice and outstretched neck, he eagerly browsed along the edge of the meat, half a foot to right and left, with incessant short and rapid snatches, which brought it away as readily as if it had been pudding. He evidently knew very well that he was stealing, but made the most of his time. The little brown dog weighed a pound or two more afterward than before.

12 December 1856, Journal *IX:179–80*

Thoreau on Dogs

MET WILLIAM WHEELER'S shaggy gray terrier, or Indian dog, going home. He got out of the road into the field and went round to avoid us.

25 December 1856, Journal *IX:198*

DINE WITH AGASSIZ at R. W. E.'s. . . . He thinks that the Esquimau dog is the only indigenous one in the United States.

20 March 1857, Journal *IX:298–99*

WENT TO WALK in the woods. When I had got half a mile or more away in the woods alone, and was sitting on a rock, was surprised to be joined by R.'s large Newfoundland dog Ranger, who had smelled me out and so tracked me. Would that I could add his woodcraft to my own! He would trot along before me as far as the winding wood-path allowed me to see him, and then, with the shortest possible glance over his shoulder, ascertain if I was following. At a fork in the road he would pause, look back at me, and deliberate which course I would take.

7 April 1857, Journal *IX:320*

WHEN M[inott] lived at Baker's, B. had a dog Lion, famous for chasing squirrels. The gray squirrels were numerous and used to run over the house sometimes. It was an old-fashioned house, slanting to one story behind, with a ladder from the roof to the ground. One day a gray squirrel ran over the house, and Lion, dashing after him up the ladder, went completely over the house and fell off the front side before he could stop, putting out one of his toes. But the squirrel did not put out any of his toes.

4 May 1857, Journal *IX:356*

To FARMER'S OWL-NEST SWAMP.

Melvin thinks there cannot be many black ducks' nests in the town, else his dog would find them, for he will follow their trail as well as another bird's, or a fox. The dog once caught five black ducks here but partly grown.

24 June 1857, Journal *IX:456*

RETURNING [from Pine Hill], I see a fox run across the road in the twilight from Potter's into Richardson's woods. He is on a canter, but I see the whitish tip of his tail. I feel a certain respect for him, because, though so large, he still maintains himself free and wild in our midst, and is so original so far as any resemblance to our race is concerned. Perhaps I like him better than his tame cousin the dog for it.

25 November 1857, Journal *X:206*

I FREQUENTLY HEAR a dog bark at some distance in the night, which, strange as it may seem, reminds me of the cooing or *crowing* of a ring dove which I heard every night a year ago at Perth Amboy. It was sure to coo on the slightest noise in the house; as good as a watch-dog. . . . The commonest and cheapest sounds, as the barking of a dog, produce the same effect on fresh and healthy ears that the rarest music does. It depends on your appetite for sound. Just as a crust is sweeter to a healthy appetite than confectionery to a pampered or diseased one. It is better that these cheap sounds be music to us than that we have the rarest ears for music in any other sense. I have lain awake at night many a time to think of the barking of a dog which I had heard long before, bathing my being again in those waves of sound, as a frequenter of the opera might lie awake remembering the music he had heard.

27 December 1857, Journal *X:226–27*

THE DOG is to the fox as the white man to the red. The former has attained to more clearness in his bark; it is more ringing and musical, more developed; he explodes the vowels of his alphabet better; and beside he has made his place so good in the world that he can run without skulking in the open field. What a smothered, ragged, feeble, and unmusical sound is the bark of the fox! It seems as if he scarcely dared raise his voice lest it should catch the ear of his tame cousin and inveterate foe.

23 January 1858, Journal *X:252–53*

WHEN I STARTED to walk that suddenly pleasant afternoon, the 28th of March, I crossed the path of the two brothers R., who were walking direct to the depot as if they had special business there that Sunday, the queer short-legged dog running ahead. . . . [One] told me how to raise a dog's dander,—any the gentlest dog's,—by looking sternly in his face and making a peculiar sound with your mouth. I then broke short the conference, continued my walk, while these gentlemen wheeled directly about and walked straight back again.

1 April 1858, Journal *X:341–42*

To BRISTER'S HILL.
. . . I heard a bark behind me, and, looking round, saw an old fox on the brow of the hill on the west side of the valley, amid the bushes, about ten rods off, looking down at me. At first it was a short, puppy-like bark, but afterward it began to bark on a higher key and more prolonged, very unlike a dog, a very ragged half-screaming *bur-ar-r-r.* . . . I was, no doubt, by the hole in which the young were. . . . It moved restlessly back and forth, or approached nearer, and stood or sat on its haunches like a dog with its tail laid out in a curve on one side, and when it barked it laid its ears flat back and stretched its nose forward. Sometimes it uttered a short, puppy-like, snappish bark.

. . . I withdrew the sooner for fear by his barking he would be betrayed to some dog or gunner.

20 May 1858, Journal X:433–37

How DOGS will resort to carrion, a dead cow or horse, half buried, no matter how stale,—the best-bred and petted village dogs, and there gorge themselves with the most disgusting offal by the hour, as if it were a season of famine! Surely they are foul creatures that we make cossets of.

18 June 1858, Journal X:499

SLIGHT AS the snow is, you are now reminded occasionally in your walks that you have contemporaries, and perchance predecessors. I see the track of a fox which was returning from his visit to a farmyard last night, and, in the wood-path, of a man and a dog. The dog must have been a large one. I see their shadows before me. In another place, where the snow is so slight and lifted up on the withered grass that no track is left, I see by the cakes or balls of snow that have dropped from his shoes that a man has passed. This would be known for a man and a dog's track in any part of the world. Five toes in a bundle, somewhat diamond-shape, forming a sort of rosette, are the print of the dog, whether on the sands of Africa or the snow of New England. The track of his master is somewhat more variable, yet reducible within certain limits.

15 November 1858, Journal XI:321–22

WE SEE THE TRACKS of a hunter and his hounds who have gone along the path from the Dell to the Cliffs. The dog makes a genuine track with his five toes, an honest dog's track, and if his master went barefoot we should count five toe-prints in his track too, and they would be seen to resemble each other remotely; but now we see only the track of a boot, and I thought the dog must be disgusted to tread in it. Walking thus where a man and two dogs had recently passed along, making a trail only a few inches wide, treading in one another's tracks alternately, the impression was that they had constantly crowded on one another, though in fact the dogs may have been a quarter of a mile ahead [of] or behind their master. The dog rosette identical [with that] which is spotted all over Greece. They go making these perfect imperfect impressions faster than a Hoe's cylinder power-press.

30 November 1858, Journal *XI:353–54*

MINOTT SAYS that a fox will lead a dog on to thin ice in order that he may get in. Tells of Jake Lakin losing a hound so, which went under the ice and was drowned below the Holt; was found afterward by Sted. Buttrick, his collar taken off and given to Lakin. They used to cross the river there on the ice, going to market, formerly.

2 January 1859, Journal *XI:387*

I HEARD LATELY the voice of a hound hunting by itself. What an awful sound to the denizens of the wood! That relentless, voracious, demonic cry, like the voice of a fiend! At hearing of which, the fox, hare, marmot, etc., tremble for their young and themselves, imagining the worst. This, however, is the sound which the lords of creation love to accompany and follow, with their bugles and "mellow horns" conveying a similar dread to the hearers instead of whispering peace to the hare's palpitating breast.

17 April 1859, Journal *XII:149*

THE SNOW having ceased falling this forenoon, I go to Holden Wood, Conantum, to look for tracks. It is too soon. I see none at all but those of a hound, and also where a partridge waded through the light snow, apparently while it was falling, making a deep gutter.

14 January 1860, Journal *XIII:89–90*

I WALK ABOUT Ripple Lake and Goose Pond. I see the old tracks of some foxes and rabbits about the edge of these ponds (over the ice) within a few feet of the shore. I think that I have noticed that animals thus commonly go round by the shore of a pond, whether for fear of the ice, or for the shelter of the shore, *i. e.* not to be seen, or because their food and game is found there. But a dog will oftener bolt straight across.

17 January 1860, Journal *XIII:94*

MINOTT SAYS that a hound which pursues a fox by scent cannot tell which way he is going; that the fox is very cunning and will often return on its track over which the dog had already run. It will ascend a high rock and then leap off very far to one side; so throw the dogs off the scent for a while and gain a breathing-spell.

22 January 1860, Journal *XIII:100–101*

WHEN A THAW COMES, old tracks are enlarged in every direction, so that an ordinary man's track will look like the track of a snow-shoe, and a hound's track will sometimes have spread to a foot in diameter (when there is a thin snow on ice), with all the toes distinct, looking like the track of a behemoth or megalonyx.

23 January 1860, Journal *XIII:103*

Thoreau on Dogs

COMING HOME LAST NIGHT in the twilight, I recognized a neighbor a dozen rods off by his walk or carriage, though it was so dark that I could not see a single feature of his person. . . .

And to-day, seeing a peculiar very long track of a man in the snow, who has been along up the river this morning, I guessed that it was George Melvin, because it was accompanied by a hound's track. . . .

We have no occasion to wonder at the instinct of a dog. In these last two instances I surpassed the instinct of the dog.

5 February 1860, Journal *XIII:127–28*

I THINK THAT the most important requisite in describing an animal, is to be sure and give its character and spirit, for in that you have, without error, the sum and effect of all its parts, known and unknown. You must tell what it is to man. Surely the most important part of an animal is its *anima*, its vital spirit, on which is based its character and all the peculiarities by which it most concerns us. Yet most scientific books which treat of animals leave this out altogether, and what they describe are as it were phenomena of dead matter. What is most interesting in a dog, for example, is his attachment to his master, his intelligence, courage, and the like, and not his anatomical structure or even many habits which affect us less.

18 February 1860, Journal *XIII:154*

I WONDER THAT the very cows and the dogs in the street do not manifest a recognition of the bright tints about and above them. I saw a terrier dog glance up and down the painted street before he turned in at his master's gate, and I wondered what he thought of those lit trees,—if they did not touch his philosophy or spirits,—but I fear he had only his common doggish thoughts after all. He trotted down the yard as if it were a matter of course after all, or else as if he deserved it all.

9 October 1860, Journal *XIV:108*

MY AUNT SOPHIA, now in her eightieth year, says that when she was a little girl my grandmother, who lived in Keene, N. H., eighty miles from Boston, went to Nova Scotia, and, in spite of all she could do, her dog Bob, a little black dog with his tail cut off, followed her to Boston, where she went aboard a vessel. Directly after, however, Bob returned to Keene. One day, Bob, lying as usual under his mistress's bed in Keene, the window being open, heard a dog bark in the street, and instantly, forgetting that he was in the second story, he sprang up and jumped out the chamber window. He came down squarely on all fours, but it surprised or shocked him so that he did not run an inch,—which greatly amused the children,—my mother and aunts.

11 March 1861, Journal *XIV:325–26*

IN WORCESTER.

Rode to east side of Quinsigamond Pond with Blake and Brown and a dry humorist, a gentleman who has been a sportsman and was well acquainted with dogs. He said that he once went by water to St. John, N. B., on a sporting excursion, taking his dog with him; but the latter had such a remarkable sense of decency that, seeing no suitable place aboard the vessel, he did not yield to the pressing demands of nature and, as the voyage lasted several days, swelled up very much. At length his master, by taking him aside and setting him the example, persuaded him to make water only. When at length he reached St. John, and was leading his dog by a rope up a long hill there which led to the town, he was compelled to stop repeatedly for his dog to empty himself and was the observed of all observers. This suggested that a dog could be educated to be far more cleanly in some respects than men are.

He also states that a fox does not regard all dogs,—or, rather, avoid them,—but only hunting dogs. He one day heard the voices of hounds in pursuit of a fox and soon after saw the fox come trotting along a path in which he himself was walking. Secreting himself behind a wall he watched the motions of the fox, wishing to get a shot at him, but at that moment his dog, a spaniel, leapt out into the path and advanced to meet the fox, which stood still without fear to receive him. They smelled of one another like dogs, and the sportsman was prevented from shooting the fox for fear of hitting his dog. So he suddenly showed himself in the path, hoping thus to separate them and get a shot. The fox immediately cantered backward in the path, but his dog ran after him so directly in a line with the fox that he was afraid to fire for fear of killing the dog.

12 May 1861, Journal *XIV:339–40*

Bonds of Affection

[ON CLARK'S ISLAND, in Plymouth Bay] Sometimes we met a wrecker with his cart and dog,—and his dog's faint bark at us wayfarers, heard through the roaring of the surf, sounded ridiculously faint. To see a little trembling dainty-footed cur stand on the margin of the ocean, and ineffectually bark at a beach-bird, amid the roar of the Atlantic! Come with design to bark at a whale, perchance! That sound will do for farmyards. All the dogs looked out of place there, naked and as if shuddering at the vastness; and I thought that they would not have been there had it not been for the countenance of their masters. . . . I used to see packs of half-wild dogs haunting the lonely beach on the south shore of Staten Island, in New York Bay, for the sake of the carrion there cast up; and I remember that once, when for a long time I had heard a furious barking in the tall grass of the marsh, a pack of half a dozen large dogs burst forth on to the beach, pursuing a little one which ran straight to me for protection, and I afforded it with some stones, though at some risk to myself; but the next day the little one was the first to bark at me. . . .

Sometimes, when I was approaching the carcass of a horse or ox which lay on the beach there, where there was no living creature in sight, a dog would unexpectedly emerge from it and slink away with a mouthful of offal.

"The Sea and the Desert," Cape Cod, *146–47*

ALL SAILORS pause to watch a steamer, and shout in welcome or derision. In one a large Newfoundland dog put his paws on the rail and stood up as high as any of them, and looked as wise. But the skipper, who did not wish to be seen no better employed than a dog, rapped him on the nose and sent him below. Such is human justice! I thought I could hear him making an effective appeal down there from human to divine justice. He must have had much the cleanest breast of the two.

"Provincetown," Cape Cod, *205*

WHEN LOOKING OVER a list of men's names in a foreign language, as of military officers, or of authors who have written on a particular subject, I am reminded once more that there is nothing in a name. The name Menschikoff, for instance, has nothing in it to my ears more human than a whisker, and it may belong to a rat. As the names of the Poles and Russians are to us, so are ours to them. It is as if they had been named by the child's rigmarole, *Iery wiery ichery van, tittle-tol-tan.* I see in my mind a herd of wild creatures swarming over the earth, and to each the herdsman has affixed some barbarous sound in his own dialect. The names of men are, of course, as cheap and meaningless as *Bose* and *Tray,* the names of dogs.

"Walking," Excursions and Poems, *236*

THOREAU ON CATS

THERE IS A TOTAL disinterestedness and self abando[n]ment vein in fretfulness and despondency, which few attain to. If there is no personality or selfishness, you may be as fretful as you please. I congratulate myself on the richness of human nature, which a virtuous and even temper had not wholly exhibited. May it not whine like a kitten or squeak like a squirrel? Some times the weakness of my fellow discovers a new suppleness, which I had not anticipated.

7 January 1841, Journal *1:218*

[IN THE MAINE WOODS] We took here a poor and leaky boat and poled up the Millinocket 2 miles to the Elder Fowler's. . . .
    . . . This house was warmed by large and complicated stoves—which struck me as rather singular— —portions of it were lined with bark— There stood the cedar broom & the pole hung high over the hearth to dry stockings &c on. Kittens were exhibited which were web-footed—and the mother was said to be part mink.

Fall 1846, Journal *2:304–5*

THE SMALL HOUSES which were scattered along the river at intervals of a mile or more, were commonly out of sight to us, but sometimes when we rowed near the shore, we heard the peevish note of a hen, or some slight domestic sound, which betrayed them. . . . I have not read of any Arcadian life which surpasses the actual luxury and serenity of these New England dwellings. . . . Sometimes there sits the brother who follows the sea, their representative man; who knows only how far it is to the nearest port, no more distances, all the rest is sea and distant capes,—patting the dog, or dandling the kitten in arms that were stretched by the cable and the oar, pulling against Boreas or the trade-winds.

"Wednesday," A Week on the Concord and Merrimack Rivers, *241–42*

SAW A CAT on the great fields—wilder than a rabbit—hunting artfully. I remember to have seen one once walking about the stoney shore at Walden Pond. It is not often that they wander so far from the houses. I once, however, met with a cat with young kittens in the woods—quite wild.

9 November 1850, Journal *3:134*

SOMEBODY shut the cat's tail in the door just now & she made such a catewaul as has driven two whole worlds out of my mind. thoughts I saw unspeakable things in the sky & looming in the horizon of my mind—and now they are all reduced to a cat's tail. Vast films of thought floated through my brain like clouds pregnant with rain enough to fertilize and restore a world— and now they are all dissipated.

16 November 1850, Journal *3:141–42*

WHAT IS A CHAMBER to which the sun does not rise in the morning? What is a chamber to which the sun does not set at evening? Such are often the chambers of the mind for the most part

Even the cat which lies on a rug all day—commences to prowl about the fields at night—resumes her ancient forest habits.— the most tenderly bred grimalkin steals forth at night. Watches some bird on its perch for an hour in the furrow like a gun at rest. She catches no cold—it is her nature. Carressed by children & cherished with a saucer of milk. Even she can erect her back & expand her tail & spit at her enemies like the wild cat of the woods. sweet sylvia

30 April 1851, Journal *3:210–11*

HOUSES NEAR THE SEA are generally low and broad. . . . The great number of windows in the ends of the houses, and their irregularity in size and position, here and elsewhere on the Cape, struck us agreeably,—as if each of the various occupants who had their *cunabula* behind had punched a hole where his necessities required it, and, according to his size and stature, without regard to outside effect. There were windows for the grown folks, and windows for the children,—three or four apiece; as a certain man had a large hole cut in his barn-door for the cat, and another smaller one for the kitten.

"The Wellfleet Oysterman," Cape Cod, *62*

THE OLD MAN said that the great clams were good to eat, but that they always took out a certain part which was poisonous, before they cooked them. "People said it would kill a cat." I did not tell him that I had eaten a large one entire that afternoon, but began to think that I was tougher than a cat.

"The Wellfleet Oysterman, Cape Cod, *67*

FULL MOON LAST NIGHT. Set out on a walk to Conantum at 7 pm. A serene evening—the sun going down behind clouds, a few white or slightly shaded piles of clouds floating in the eastern sky—but a broad clear mellow cope left for the moon to rise into— An evening for poets to describe. . . . All nature is in an expectant attitude— Before Goodwin's House—at the opening of the Sudbury Road The swallows are diving at a tortoise shell cat who curvets & frisks rather awkwardly as if she did not know whether to be scared or not—

14 June 1851, Journal *3:264*

THE POET IS A MAN who lives at last by watching his moods. An old poet comes at last to watch his moods as narrowly as a cat does a mouse.

28 August 1851, Journal *4:16*

8 ½ AM UP THE RIVER in a boat to Pelham's Pond with W. E[llery] C[hanning]
 . . . The pup nibbles clams, or plays with a bone no matter how dry — Thus the dog can be taken on a river Voyage—but the cat cannot. she is too set in her ways.

15 October 1851, Journal *4:147, 149–50*

DAY BEFORE YESTERDAY I saw the hunters out with a dozen dogs—but only 2 pussies one white & one little gray one did I see—for so many men & dogs who seem to set all the village a-stir, as if the fox's trail led through it.

29 January 1852, Journal *4:303*

⌈T⌉HE DOG commonly is not put to any use. Cats catch mice; but dogs only worry the cats.

"Quebec and Montmorenci," A Yankee in Canada,
in Excursions and Poems, *30*

THE MASTER OF THE HOUSE, in his long-pointed red woolen cap, had a thoroughly antique physiognomy of the old Norman stamp. He might have come over with Jacques Cartier. His was the hardest French to understand of any we had heard yet, for there was a great difference between one speaker and another, and this man talked with a pipe in his mouth beside,—a kind of tobacco French. I asked him what he called his dog. He shouted *Brock!* (the name of the breed). We like to hear the cat called *min,* "Min! min! min!"

"St. Anne," A Yankee in Canada, *in* Excursions and Poems, *50*

HAVING FOUND MY WAY by an obscure passage near the St. Louis Gate to the glacis on the north of the citadel proper,—I believe that I was the only visitor then in the city who got in there,—I enjoyed a prospect nearly as good as from within the citadel itself, which I had explored some days before. As I walked on the glacis I heard the sound of a bagpipe from the soldiers' dwellings in the rock, and was further soothed and affected by the sight of a soldier's cat walking up a cleated plank into a high loop-hole designed for *mus-catry,* as serene as Wisdom herself, and with a gracefully waving motion of her tail, as if her ways were ways of pleasantness and all her paths were peace.

"The Walls of Quebec," A Yankee in Canada,
in Excursions and Poems, *73*

WHAT AILS the Pewee's tail?— It is loosely hung. — pulsating with life. What mean these wag tail birds? Cats & dogs too express some of their life through their tails.

2 April 1852, Journal *4:416*

THE FARM HOUSES under their shady trees (Baker's) look as if the inhabitants were taking their siesta at this hour. . . . Why does work go forward now? No scouring of tubs or cans now.— The cat and all are gone to sleep preparing for an early tea—excepting the indefatigable never resting hoers in the corn field—who have carried a jug of molasses & water to the field & will ring their shirts tonight.

15 June 1852, Journal *5:98*

CAT

"prolific hybrids have been produced by the union of animals generically distinct, between the martin, (Mustela martes) and the domestic cat."

Transcribed from Richard Harlan, Fauna Americana *(1825)*,
Thoreau's Fact Book, 1:120–21

WHEN YESTERDAY Sophia & I were rowing past Mr Pritchards Land where the river is bordered by a row of elms & low willows at 6 Pm—we heard a singular note of distress as it were from a cat bird. a loud vibrating cat bird sort of note—as if the cat birds mew were imitated by a smart vibrating spring. Blackbirds & others were flitting about apparently attracted by it— At first thinking it was merely some peevish catbird or red-wing—I was disregarding it but on 2nd thought turned the bows to the shore—looking into the trees as well as over the shore—thinking some bird might be in distress—caught by a snake or in a forked twig. The hovering birds dispersed at my approached—the note of distress sounded louder & nearer as I approached the shore covered with low osiers— The sound came from the ground not from the trees— I saw a little black animal making haste to meet the boat under the osiers—a young muskrat—? —a mink?—no it was a little dot of a kitten It was scarcely 6 inches long from the face to the base—or I might as well say the tip of the tail—for the latter was a short sharp pyramid perfectly perpendicular—but not swelled in the least— It was a very handsome and very precocious kitten—in perfectly good condition—its breadth being considerably more than 1/3 of its length. Ceasing its mewing it came scrambling over the stones as fast as its weak legs would permit straight to me. I took it up & dropped it into the boat—but while I was pushing off it ran the length of the boat to Sophia—who held it while we rowed homeward. Evidently it had not been weaned—was smaller than we remembered that kittens ever were—almost infinitely small— Yet it had hailed a boat—its life being in danger & sailed itself. Its performance, considering its age & amount of experience was more wonderful than that of any young mathematician or musician that I have read of. Various were the conjectures as to how the kitten came there—a quarter of a mile from a house— The possible solutions were finally reduced to three 1st It must either have been born there or 2ndly carried there by its mother—or 3dly by human hands. In the first case it had possibly brothers & sisters one or both & its mother had left them to go a hunting on her own account—& might be expected back— — In the 2nd she might equally be expected to return. At any rate not having thought of all this till we got home we found that we had got our selves into a scrape— For this kitten though exceedingly interesting required one nurse to

attend it constantly for the present & of course another to spell
the first—and beside we had already a cat well nigh grown who
manifested such a disposition toward the young stranger that
we had no doubt it would have torne it in pieces in a moment
if left alone with it. As nobody made up his or her mind to
have it drowned & still less to drown it—having once looked
into its innocent extremely pale blue eyes—(as of milk thrice
skimed) and had his finger or his chin sucked by it—while its
eyes being shut its little paws played a soothing tune—it was
resolved to keep it till it could be suitably disposed of. It rested
nowhere in no lap—under no covert—but still faintly cryed for
its mother & its accustomed supper—it ran toward every sound
or movement of a human being and who ever crossed the room
it was sure to follow at a rapid pace.— It had all the ways of a
cat of the maturest years could purr divinely & raised its back
to rub at boots & shoes When it raised its foot to scratch its
ear which by the way it never hit, it was sure to fall over & roll
on the floor— It climbed straight up the sitter faintly mewing
all the way & sucked his chin— In vain at first its head was
bent down into saucers of milk which its eyes did not see & its
chin was wetted— But soon it learned to suck a finger that had
been dipped in it—& better still a rag. & then at last it slept &
rested. The street was explored in vain to find its owner, but in
vain—& at length an Irish family took it into their cradle. Soon
after we learned that a neighbor who had heard the mewing
of kittens in the partition had sent for a carpenter taken off a
board & found 2 the very day at noon that we sailed. That same
hour it was first brought to the light a coarse Irish cook had vol-
unteered to drown it—had carried it to the river & without bag
or sinker had cast it in. It saved itself & hailed a boat!— What
an eventful life—what a precocious kitten. We feared it owed its
first plump condition to the water— How strong & effective the
instinct of self-preservation.

22 May 1853, Journal *6:143–45*

Thoreau on Cats

WHEN I WAS AT C[hanning]'s the other evening, he punched his cat with the poker because she purred too loud for him.

PM TO CLINTONIA SWAMP & POND

Saw a black snake dead 4 feet 3 inches long slate-colored beneath. Saw what was called a California Cat which a colored man brought home from California. An animal at least a third smaller than a cat & shaped more like a pole-cat or weasel. brown-grey with a catlike tail of alternate black-& white rings— very large ears & eyes which were prominent, long body like a weasel & sleeps with its head between its fore paws—curling itself about—a rank smell to it— It was lost several days in our woods & was caught again in a tree about a crow's nest.

I HAD ALREADY BOUGHT the shanty of James Collins, an Irishman who worked on the Fitchburg Railroad, for boards. James Collins' shanty was considered an uncommonly fine one. . . . Mrs. C. came to the door and asked me to view it from the inside. . . . In her own words, they were "good boards overhead, good boards all around, and a good window,"—of two whole squares originally, only the cat had passed out that way lately. . . . The bargain was soon concluded, for James had in the mean while returned. I to pay four dollars and twenty-five cents to-night, he to vacate at five to-morrow morning, selling to nobody else meanwhile: I to take possession at six. . . . At six I passed him and his family on the road. One large bundle held their all,—bed, coffee-mill, looking-glass, hens,—all but the cat, she took to the woods and became a wild cat, and, as I learned afterward, trod in a trap set for woodchucks, and so became a dead cat at last.

"Building the House," Walden, *42–44*

ONCE I WAS SURPRISED to see a cat walking along the stony shore of the pond, for they rarely wander so far from home. The surprise was mutual. Nevertheless the most domestic cat, which has lain on a rug all her days, appears quite at home in the woods, and, by her sly and stealthy behavior, proves herself more native there than the regular inhabitants. Once, when berrying, I met with a cat with young kittens in the woods, quite wild, and they all, like their mother, had their backs up and were fiercely spitting at me. A few years before I lived in the woods there was what was called a "winged cat" in one of the farm-houses in Lincoln nearest the pond, Mr. Gilian Baker's. When I called to see her in June, 1842, she was gone a-hunting in the woods, as was her wont, (I am not sure whether it was a male or female, and so use the more common pronoun,) but her mistress told me that she came into the neighborhood a little more than a year before, in April, and was finally taken into their house; that she was of a dark brownish-gray color, with a white spot on her throat, and white feet, and had a large bushy tail like a fox; that in the winter the fur grew thick and flatted out along her sides, forming strips ten or twelve inches long by two and a half wide, and under her chin like a muff, the upper side loose, the under matted like felt, and in the spring these appendages dropped off. They gave me a pair of her "wings," which I keep still. There is no appearance of a membrane about them. Some thought it was part flying-squirrel or some other wild animal, which is not impossible, for, according to naturalists, prolific hybrids have been produced by the union of the marten and domestic cat. This would have been the right kind of cat for me to keep, if I had kept any; for why should not a poet's cat be winged as well as his horse?

"Brute Neighbors," Walden, *232–33 (see also 9 November 1850 and 30 April 1851,* Journal *3:134 and 3:210–11)]*

Thoreau on Cats

ONE AFTERNOON I amused myself by watching a barred owl (*Strix nebulosa*) sitting on one of the lower dead limbs of a white-pine, close to the trunk, in broad daylight, I standing within a rod of him. He could hear me when I moved and cronched the snow with my feet, but could not plainly see me. When I made most noise he would stretch out his neck, and erect his neck feathers, and open his eyes wide; but their lids soon fell again, and he began to nod. I too felt a slumberous influence after watching him half an hour, as he sat thus with his eyes half open, like a cat, winged brother of the cat. There was only a narrow slit left between their lids, by which he preserved a peninsular relation to me; thus, with half-shut eyes, looking out from the land of dreams, and endeavoring to realize me, vague object or mote that interrupted his visions. At length, on some louder noise or my nearer approach, he would grow uneasy and sluggishly turn about on his perch, as if impatient at having his dreams disturbed; and when he launched himself off and flapped through the pines, spreading his wings to unexpected breadth, I could not hear the slightest sound from them. Thus, guided amid the pine boughs rather by a delicate sense of their neighborhood than by sight, feeling his twilight way as it were with his sensitive pinions, he found a new perch, where he might in peace await the dawning of his day.

"Winter Visitors," Walden, 266

IT IS NOT WORTH the while to go round the world to count the cats in Zanzibar.

"Conclusion," Walden, 322

PADDLED TO BAKER FARM just after sundown, by full moon.

I suppose this is the Harvest Moon, since the sun must be in Virgo, enters Libra the 23d *inst.*

The wind has gone down, and it is a still, warm night, and no mist.

It is just after sundown. The moon not yet risen, one star, Jupiter (?), visible, and many bats over and about our heads, and small skaters creating a myriad dimples on the evening waters. We see a muskrat crossing, and pass a white cat on the shore. There are many clouds about and a beautiful sunset sky, a yellowish (dunnish?) golden sky, between them in the horizon, looking up the river. All this is reflected in the water. The beauty of the sunset is doubled by the reflection. . . . This seems the first autumnal sunset. The small skaters seem more active than by day, or their slight dimpling is more obvious in the lit twilight. A stray white cat sits on the shore looking over the water. This is her hour. A nighthawk dashes past, low over the water. This is what we had.

7 September 1854, Journal *VII:19-20*

I AM [reading] William Wood's "New England's Prospect."

.   .   .

Of quadrupeds no longer found in Concord, he names the lion,—that Cape Ann Lion "which some affirm that they have seen," which may have been a cougar, for he adds, "Plimouth men have traded for Lions skins in former times,"—bear, moose, deer, porcupines, "the grim-fac'd Ounce, and rav'nous howling Wolf," and beaver. Martens.

.   .   .

I do not know whether his ounce or wild cat is the Canada lynx or wolverine. He calls it wild cat and does not describe the little wildcat. (*Vide* Indian book.) Says they are accounted "very good meat. Their skins be a very deep kind of fur, spotted white and black on the belly." Audubon and Bachman make the *Lynx rufus* black and white beneath.

24 January 1855, Journal *VII:132–35*

THE COLDEST NIGHT for a long, long time was last. Sheets froze stiff about the faces. Cat mewed to have the door opened, but was at first disinclined to go out. When she came in at nine she smelt of meadow-hay. We all took her up and smelled of her, it was so fragrant. Had cuddled in some barn. People dreaded to go to bed. The ground cracked in the night as if a powder-mill had blown up, and the timbers of the house also.

7 February 1855, Journal *VII:173*

ANOTHER RATHER WARM morning, still more overcast than yesterday's. . . .

Aunt Louisa says that her cousin Nahum Jones, son to that Nathan whom her mother and sisters visited with her down east, carried a cat to the West Indies, sold his vessel there; and though the same vessel did not return, and he came back in another vessel without the cat, the cat got home to Gouldsboro somehow, unaccountably, about the same time that he did. Captain Woodard told her that he carried the same cat three times round the world.

14 February 1855, Journal *VII:185*

ALL DAY a steady, warm, imprisoning rain carrying off the snow, not unmusical on my roof. It is a rare time for the student and reader who cannot go abroad in the afternoon, provided he can keep awake, for we are wont to be drowsy as cats in such weather. Without, it is not walking but wading. . . . It seems like a distant forerunner of spring.

15 February 1855, Journal *VII:186*

THE STRIPED SQUIRREL is the smallest quadruped that we commonly notice in our walks in the woods, and we do not realize, especially in summer, when their tracks are not visible, that the aisles of the wood are threaded by countless wild mice, and no more that the meadows are swarming in many places with meadow mice and moles. The cat brings in a mole from time to time, and we see where they have heaved up the soil in the meadow. We see the tracks of mice on the snow in the woods, or once in a year one glances by like a flash through the grass or ice at our feet, and that is for the most part all that we see of them.

20 February 1855, Journal *VII:201–2*

MINOTT says that Messer tells him he saw a striped squirrel (!) yesterday. His cat caught a mole lately, not a star-nosed one, but one of those that heave up the meadow. She sometimes catches a little dark-colored mouse with a sharp nose.

24 February 1855, Journal *VII:211*

HUMPHREY BUTTRICK, one of eight who alone returned from Texas out of twenty-four. . . . [f]ound in a hen-hawk's nest once the legs of a cat.

3 May 1855, Journal *VII:353*

THE SEA THUS PLAYS with the land holding a sand-bar in its mouth awhile before it swallows it, as a cat plays with a mouse; but the fatal gripe is sure to come at last.

"The Highland Light," Cape Cod, *122*

P. M.—TO HILL BY ASSABET.

This forenoon the boys found a little black kitten about a third grown on the Island or Rock, but could not catch it. We supposed that some one had cast it in to drown it. This afternoon, as I was paddling by the Island, I saw what I thought a duck swimming down the river diagonally, to the south shore just below the grassy island, opposite the rock; then I thought it two ducks, then a muskrat. It passed out of sight round a bend. I landed and walked alongshore, and found that it was a kitten, which had just got ashore. It was quite wet excepting its back. It swam quite rapidly, the whole length of its back out, but was carried down about as fast by the stream. It had probably first crossed from the rock to the grassy island, and then from the lower end of this to the town side of the stream, on which side it may have been attracted by the noise of the town. It was rather weak and staggered as it ran, from starvation or cold, being wet, or both. A very pretty little black kitten.

4 November 1855, Journal *VIII:5*

A COLD, GRAY DAY, once spitting snow. Water froze in tubs enough to bear last night.

Minott had two cats on his knee. One given away without his knowledge a fortnight before had just found its way back. He says he would not kill a cat for twenty dollars,—no, not for fifty. Finally he told his women folks that he would not do it for five hundred, or any sum. He thought they loved life as well as we. Johnny Vose would n't do it. He used to carry down milk to a shop every day for a litter of kittens.

19 November 1855, Journal *VIII:31*

MET THERIEN coming from Lincoln on the railroad. He says that he carried a cat from Jacob Baker's to Riordan's shanty in a bag in the night, but she ran home again. "Had they not a cat in the shanty?" I asked. "Yes," said he, "but she was run over by the cars and killed; they found her head on the track separated from her body, just below the pond." That cat of Baker's used to eat eggs and so he wished to get rid of her. He carried her in a bag to Waltham, but she came back.

8 December 1855, Journal *VIII:40*

J. FARMER SAYS that he once tried to kill a cat by taking her by the legs and striking her head against a stone, but she made off, and in a week was about again, apparently as well as ever, and he did not meddle with her again.

18 December 1855, Journal *VIII:52–53*

THINK OF THE LIFE of a kitten, ours for instance: last night her eyes set in a fit, doubtful if she will ever come out of it, and she is set away in a basket and submitted to the recuperative powers of nature; this morning running up the clothes-pole and erecting her back in frisky sport to every passer.

23 December 1855, Journal *VIII:60*

THE SNOW is so light in the swamps under the crust, amid the andromeda, that a cat could almost run there. There are but few tracks of mice, now the snow is so deep. They run underneath.

30 January 1856, Journal *VIII:154*

OUR KITTEN Min, two-thirds grown, was playing with Sophia's broom this morning, as she was sweeping the parlor, when she suddenly went into a fit, dashed round the room, and, the door being opened, rushed up two flights of stairs and leaped from the attic window to the ice and snow by the side of the door-step,—a descent of a little more than twenty feet,—passed round the house and was lost. But she made her appearance again about noon, at the window, quite well and sound in every joint, even playful and frisky.

1 February 1856, Journal *VIII:158*

OUR YOUNG MALTESE CAT Min, which has been absent five cold nights, the ground covered deep with crusted snow,—her first absence,—and given up for dead, has at length returned at daylight, awakening the whole house with her mewing and afraid of the strange girl we have got in the meanwhile. She is a mere wrack of skin and bones, with a sharp nose and wiry tail. She is as one returned from the dead. There is as much rejoicing as at the return of the prodigal son, and if we had a fatted calf we should kill it. Various are the conjectures as to her adventures,—whether she has had a fit, been shut up somewhere, or lost, torn in pieces by a certain terrier or frozen to death. In the meanwhile she is fed with the best that the house affords, minced meats and saucers of warmed milk, and, with the aid of unstinted sleep in all laps in succession, is fast picking up her crumbs. She has already found her old place under the stove, and is preparing to make a stew of her brains there.

28 February 1856, Journal *VIII:192–93*

P. M.—To Lee's Cliff by boat.

· · ·

. . . It is worth the while to go there to smell the catnep. I always bring some home for the cat at this season.

18 April 1856, Journal *VIII:292–93*

Dor-bugs hum in the yard,—and were heard against the windows some nights ago. The cat is springing into the air for them.

23 May 1856, Journal *VIII:354*

Heard of, and sought out, the hut of Martha Simons, the only pure-blooded Indian left about New Bedford. She lives alone on the narrowest point of the Neck, near the shore, in sight of New Bedford. . . .

She was born on that spot. Her grandfather also lived on the same spot, though not in the same house. He was the last of her race who could speak Indian. She had heard him pray in Indian, but could only understand "Jesus Christ." Her only companion was a miserable tortoise-shell kitten which took no notice of us.

26 June 1856, Journal *VIII:390–91*

THE MOST INTERESTING sight I saw in Brattleboro was the skin and skull of a panther (*Felis concolor*) (cougar, catamount, painter, American lion, puma). . . . This creature was very catlike, though the tail was not tapering, but as large at the extremity as anywhere, yet not tufted like the lion's. It had a long neck, a long thin body, like a lean cat. Its fore feet were about six inches long by four or five wide, as set up.

9 September 1856, Journal *IX:71–72*

IN ANOTHER ARTICLE, of May, 1855, on "The Lion and his Kind," the animals are placed in this order: the domestic cat, wildcat, the ocelot or tiger-cat of Peru and Mexico, the caracal of Asia and Africa, the lynx of North America, the chetah of India and Africa, the ounce of India (perhaps a rough variety of the leopard), the leopard, the jaguar, the cougar, the tiger, the lion. "The Cougar is the American lion—at least it bears a closer resemblance to that noble brute than any other of the feline family, for it is destitute of the stripes of the tiger, the spots of the leopard, and the rosettes of the jaguar; but when full-grown possesses a tawny-red color, almost uniform over the whole body, and hence the inference that it is like the lion." "Cougar is a corruption of the Mexican name." Ranges between Paraguay and the Great Lakes of North America. "In form it is less attractive than the generality of its species, there being an apparent want of symmetry; for it is observable that its back is hollow, its legs short and thick, and its tail does not gracefully taper; yet nature has invested the cougar with other qualities as a compensation, the most remarkable of which is an apparent power to render itself quite invisible; for so cunningly tinged is its fur, that it perfectly mingles with the bark of trees—in fact, with all subdued tints—and stretched upon a limb, or even extended upon the floor of its dimly lighted cage, you must prepare your eye by considerable mental resolution to be assured of its positive presence." Its flesh is eaten by some. Mrs. Jane Swisshelm kept one which grew to be nine feet long, and, according to her, in this writer's words, "If in exceeding good-humor he would purr; but if he wished to intimidate, he would raise his back, erect his hair, and spit like a cat. In the twilight of the evening the animal was accustomed to pace back and forth to the full extent of his limits, ever and anon uttering a short, piercing shriek, which made the valley reverberate for half a mile or more in every direction. Mrs. Swisshelm says these sounds were the shrillest, and at the same time the most mournful she ever heard. They might, perhaps, be likened to the scream of a woman in an agony of terror." He once sprang at her, but was brought up by his chain. When preparing to spring, his eyes were "green and blazing, and the tip of his tail moving from side to side." This paper describes "a full-grown royal tiger, measuring four feet seven inches from the nose to the insertion of the tail. . . . Unlike the miserable wretches we see in our menageries, etc." The Brattleboro paper makes the panther four feet eleven inches, so measured!!

4 October 1856, Journal *IX:100–102*

SEVERAL INCHES OF SNOW, but a rather soft and mild air still. Now see the empty chalices of the blue-curls and the rich brown-fruited pinweed above the crust. (The very cat was full of spirits this morning, rushing about and frisking on the snow-crust, which bore her alone. When I came home from New Jersey the other day, was struck with the sudden growth and stateliness of our cat Min,—his cheeks puffed out like a regular grimalkin. I suspect it is a new coat of fur against the winter chiefly. The cat is a third bigger than a month ago, like a patriarch wrapped in furs; and a mouse a day, I hear, is nothing to him now.) This as I go through the Depot Field, where the stub ends of corn-stalks rise above the snow. I find half a dozen russets, touched and discolored within by frost, still hanging on Wheeler's tree by the wall.

30 November 1856, Journal *IX:141*

S OPHIA SAYS that just before I came home Min caught a mouse and was playing with it in the yard. It had got away from her once or twice, and she had caught it again; and now it was steal-ing off again, as she lay complacently watching it with her paws tucked under her, when her friend Riordan's stout but solitary cock stepped up inquisitively, looked down at it with one eye, turning his head, then picked it up by the tail and gave it two or three whacks on the ground, and giving it a dexterous toss into the air, caught it in its open mouth, and it went head fore-most and alive down his capacious throat in the twinkling of an eye, never again to be seen in this world, Min, all the while, with paws comfortably tucked under her, looking on uncon-cerned. What matters it one mouse more or less to her? The cock walked off amid the currant bushes, stretched his neck up, and gulped once or twice, and the deed was accomplished, and then he crowed lustily in celebration of the exploit. It might be set down among the *gesta* (if not *digesta*) *Gallorum*. There were several human witnesses. It is a question whether Min ever understood where that mouse went to. Min sits composedly sentinel, with paws tucked under her, a good part of her days at present, by some ridiculous little hole, the possible entryway of a mouse. She has a habit of stretching or sharpening her claws on all smooth hair-bottomed chairs and sofas, greatly to my mother's vexation.

4 December 1856, Journal *IX:154–55*

I WALKED up & down the Main Street at half past 5 in the dark.
. . . You little dream who is occupying Worcester when you are
all asleep. Several things occurred there that night, which I will
venture to say were not put into the Transcript. A cat caught
a mouse at the depot, & gave it to her kitten to play with. So
that world famous tragedy goes on by night as well as by day, &
nature is *emphatically* wrong.

Letter to H. G. O. Blake, 6 December 1856, Correspondence, *443*

WONDERFUL, wonderful is our life and that of our companions! That there should be such a thing as a brute animal, not
human! and that it should attain to a sort of society with our
race! Think of cats, for instance. They are neither Chinese nor
Tartars. They do not go to school, nor read the Testament; yet
how near they come to doing so! how much they are like us who
do so! What sort of philosophers are we, who know absolutely
nothing of the origin and destiny of cats? At length, without
having solved any of these problems, we fatten and kill and eat
some of our cousins!

12 December 1856, Journal *IX:178–79*

AT LEE'S CLIFF I pushed aside the snow with my foot and got
some fresh green catnip for Min.

25 December 1856, Journal *IX:198*

TO-DAY I see Parker is out with horse and cart, collecting dead
wood at the Rock and drawing it home over the meadow. I saw
the English servant-girl with one of the children flat on the ice
hard at work on the river cutting a hole with a hatchet, but, as
the ice was thick and the water gushed up too soon for her, I

saw that she would fail and directed her to an open place. She was nearly beat out. The hole, she said, was to drown a cat in; probably one which the W——s left behind as they did Parker. E—— is resolved on a general clearing-up.

2 January 1857, Journal *IX:204*

MISS MINOTT tells me that she does not think her brother George has ever been to Boston more than once (though she tells me he says he has been twice), and certainly not since 1812. . . . Minott says he has lived where he now does as much as sixty years. He has not been up in town for three years, on account of his rheumatism. Does nothing whatever in the house but read the newspapers and few old books they have, the Almanac especially, and hold the cats, and very little indeed out of the house. Is just able to saw and split the wood.

8 January 1857, Journal *IX:212–13*

AM AGAIN SURPRISED to see a song sparrow sitting for hours on our wood-pile in the yard, in the midst of snow in the yard. It is unwilling to move. People go to the pump, and the cat and dog walk round the wood-pile without starting it. I examine it at my leisure through a glass. Remarkable that the coldest of all winters these summer birds should remain.

28 January 1857, Journal *IX:233*

FOR TWO NIGHTS PAST it has not frozen, but a thick mist has overhung the earth, and you awake to the unusual and agreeable sight of water in the streets. Several strata of snow have been washed away from the drifts, down to that black one formed when dust was blowing from plowed fields.

Riordan's solitary cock, standing on such an icy snow-heap, feels the influence of the softened air, and the steam from patches of bare ground here and there, and has found his voice again. The warm air has thawed the music in his throat, and he crows lustily and unweariedly, his voice rising to the last. Yesterday morning our feline Thomas, also feeling the spring-like influence, stole away along the fences and walls, which raise him above the water, and only returned this morning reeking with wet. Having got his breakfast, he already stands on his hind legs, looking wishfully through the window, and, the door being opened a little, he is at once off again in spite of the rain.

8 February 1857, Journal *IX:245*

[AT SITE OF the Lee house (ca. 1650)] A boy who was at the fire said to me, "This was the chimney in which the cat was burned up; she ran into a stove, and we heard her cries in the midst of the fire." Parker says there was no cat; she was drowned.

16 February 1857, Journal *IX:264*

MINOTT always sits in the corner behind the door, close to the stove, with commonly the cat by his side, often in his lap. Often he sits with his hat on.

20 February 1857, Journal *IX:274*

AT THE PILGRIM HOUSE [in Provincetown, Massachusetts], though it was not crowded, they put me into a small attic cham-ber which had two double beds in it, and only one window, high in a corner, twenty and a half inches by twenty-five and a half, in the alcove when it was swung open, and it required a chair to look out conveniently. Fortunately it was not a cold night and the window could be kept open, though at the risk of being visited by the cats, which appear to swarm on the roofs of Provincetown like the mosquitoes on the summits of its hills. I have spent four memorable nights there in as many different years, and have added considerable thereby to my knowledge of the natural history of the cat and the bedbug. Sleep was out of the question. A night in one of the attics of Provincetown! to say nothing of what is to be learned in entomology. It would be worth the while to send a professor there, one who was also skilled in entomology. Such is your *Pilgerruhe* or Pilgrims'-Rest. Every now and then one of these animals on its travels leaped from a neighboring roof on to mine, with such a noise as if a six-pounder had fallen within two feet of my head,—the discharge of a catapult,—a twelve-pounder discharged by a catapult,—and then followed such a scrambling as banished sleep for a long season, while I watched lest they came in at the open window. A kind of foretaste, methought, of the infernal regions. I did n't wonder they gave quit-claim deeds of their land here. My experience is that you fare best at private houses. The barroom may be defined a place to spit.

> "Soon as the evening shades prevail,
> The *cats take* up the wondrous tale."

At still midnight, when, half awake, half asleep, you seem to be weltering in your own blood on a battle-field, you hear the stealthy tread of padded feet belonging to some animal of the cat tribe, perambulating the roof within a few inches of your head.

21 June 1857, Journal *IX:452–53*

THERE HAS BEEN, amid the chips where a wood-pile stood, in our yard, a bumblebee's nest for ten days or more. Near it there was what I should have called a mouse's nest of withered grass, but this was mainly of different material and *perhaps* was made by the bee. It was a little heap two inches high, six long, and four wide, made of old withered grass and *small bits* of rags, brown paper, cotton-wool, strings, lint, and whole feathers, with a small half-closed hole at one end, at which the ⌈bee⌉ buzzed and showed himself if you touched the nest. I saw the cat putting out her paw there and starting back, and to-day I find the remains, apparently, of the bee dead at the entrance. On opening, I find nothing in the nest.

5 July 1857, Journal *IX:469–70*

THE RESTLESS OCEAN may at any moment cast up a whale or a wrecked vessel at your feet. . . . No creature could move slowly where there was so much life around. The few wreckers were either going or coming, and the ships and the sand-pipers, and the screaming gulls overhead; nothing stood still but the shore. . . . Sometimes we met a wrecker with his cart and dog,—and his dog's faint bark at us wayfarers, heard through the roaring of the surf, sounded ridiculously faint. To see a little trembling dainty-footed cur stand on the margin of the ocean, and ineffectually bark at a beach-bird, amid the roar of the Atlantic! Come with design to bark at a whale, perchance! That sound will do for farmyards. All the dogs looked out of place there, naked and as if shuddering at the vastness; and I thought that they would not have been there had it not been for the countenance of their masters. Still less could you think of a cat bending her steps that way, and shaking her wet foot over the Atlantic; yet even this happens sometimes, they tell me.

"The Sea and the Desert," Cape Cod, *145–46*

A CLEAR, COLD, windy afternoon. The cat crackles with electricity when you stroke her, and the fur rises up to your touch.

25 November 1857, Journal *X:202*

SPOKE TO Skinner about that wildcat which he says he heard a month ago in Ebby Hubbard's woods. He was going down to Walden in the evening, to see if geese had not settled in it (with a companion), when they heard this sound, which his companion at first thought made by a coon, but S. said no, it was a wildcat. He says he has heard them often in the Adirondack region, where he has purchased furs. He told him he would hear it again soon, and he did. Somewhat like the domestic cat, a low sort of growling and then a sudden quick-repeated caterwaul, or *yow yow yow*, or *yang yang yang*. He says they utter this from time to time when on the track of some prey.

28 November 1857, Journal *X:212–13*

I HEAR a characteristic anecdote respecting Mrs. Hoar, from good authority. Her son Edward, who takes his father's place and attends to the same duties, asked his mother the other night, when about retiring, "Shall I put the cat down cellar?" "No," said she, "you may put her outdoors." The next night he asked, "Shall I put the cat outdoors?" "No," answered she, "you may put her down cellar." The third night he asked, "Shall I put the cat down cellar or outdoors?" "Well," said his mother, "you may open the cellar door and then open the front door, and let her go just which way she pleases." Edward suggested that it was a cold night for the cat to be outdoors, but his mother said, "Who knows but she has a little kitten somewhere to look after?" Mrs. H. is a peculiar woman, who has her own opinion and way, a strong-willed, managing woman.

13 December 1857, Journal *X:223*

To Cambridge and Boston.
Saw, at a menagerie, a Canada lynx, said to have been taken at the White Mountains. It looked much like a monstrous gray cat standing on stilts, with its tail cut down to five inches, a tuft of hair on each ear and a ruff under the throat.

15 February 1858, Journal X:283

How they got a cat up there [at Ansell Smith's house at Chesuncook Lake] I do not know, for they are as shy as my aunt about entering a canoe. I wondered that she did not run up a tree on the way; but perhaps she was bewildered by the very crowd of opportunities.

"Chesuncook," The Maine Woods, *127–28*

The cat sleeps on her head! What does this portend? It is more alarming than a dozen comets. How long prejudice survives! The big-bodied fisherman asks me doubtingly about the comet seen these nights in the northwest,—if there is any danger to be apprehended from that side! I would fain suggest that only he is dangerous to himself.

1 October 1858, Journal XI:191

The garden is alive with migrating sparrows these mornings. The cat comes in from an early walk amid the weeds. She is full of sparrows and wants no more breakfast this morning, unless it be a saucer of milk, the dear creature. I saw her studying ornithology between the corn-rows.

2 October 1858, Journal XI:191

Bonds of Affection

ONE BRINGS ME this morning a Carolina rail alive, this year's
bird evidently from its marks. He saved it from a cat in the road
near the Battle-Ground.

3 October 1858, Journal *XI:192*

6:30 A. M.—VERY HARD FROST these mornings; the grasses,
to their finest branches, clothed with it.

The cat comes stealthily creeping towards some prey amid
the withered flowers in the garden, which being disturbed by
my approach, she runs low toward it with an unusual glare or
superficial light in her eye, ignoring her oldest acquaintance, as
wild as her remotest ancestor; and presently I see the first tree
sparrow hopping there. I hear them also amid the alders by the
river, singing sweetly,—but a few notes.

29 October 1858, Journal *XI:259*

WHEN THE PLAYFUL BREEZE drops on the pool, it springs to
right and left, quick as a kitten playing with dead leaves, clapping her paw on them. Sometimes it merely raises a single wave
at one point, as if a fish darted near the surface.

9 April 1859, Journal *XII:130*

THE OTHER DAY a tender-hearted man came to the depot and
informed Neighbor Wild that there was a Maltese cat caught
in a steel trap near the depot, which perhaps was his. Wild
thought it must be his or "Min Thoreau." She had tried to jump
over a fence with the trap on her leg, but had lodged one side
while the trap hung the other. The man could not stand to open
the trap, the cat scratched so, but at length he threw the trap
over, and so the cat went home, dragging it to Wild's (for it was

his cat), and the man advised him to keep the trap to pay the one who set it for his inhumanity. I suspect, however, that the cat had wandered off to Swamp Bridge Brook and there trod in a trap set for mink or the like. It is a wonder it does not happen oftener.

I saw a star-nosed mole dead in the path on Conantum yesterday, with no obvious wound.

12 September 1859, Journal *XII:322–23*

As the lion is said to lie in a thicket or in tall reeds and grass by day, slumbering, and sallies at night, just so with the cat. She will ensconce herself for the day in the grass or weeds in some out-of-the-way nook near the house, and arouse herself toward night.

28 September 1859, Journal *XII:357*

In the midst of Ledum Swamp I came upon a white cat under the spruces and the water brush, which evidently had not seen me till I was within ten feet. There she stood, quite still, as if hoping to be concealed, only turning her head slowly away from and toward me, looking at me thus two or three times with an extremely worried expression in her eyes, but not moving any other part of her body. It occurred to me from her peculiar anxious expression and this motion, as if spellbound, that perhaps she was deaf; but when I moved toward her she found the use of her limbs and dashed off, bounding over the andromeda by successive leaps like a rabbit, no longer making her way through or beneath it.

15 November 1859, Journal *XII:444*

WE CANNOT SPARE the very lively and lifelike descriptions of some of the old naturalists. They sympathize with the creatures which they describe. . . .

Though some beasts are described in this book [Edward Topsell's 1607 translation of Conrad Gesner—*The History of Four-footed Beasts*] which have no existence as I can learn but in the imagination of the writers, they really have an existence there, which is saying not a little, for most of our modern authors have not imagined the actual beasts which they presume to describe. . . .

These men had an adequate idea of a beast, or what a beast should be, a very *bellua* (the translator makes the word *bestia* to be "*a vastando*"); and they will describe and will draw you a cat with four strokes, more beastly or beast-like to look at than Mr. Ruskin's favorite artist draws a tiger. They had an adequate idea of the wildness of beasts and of men, and in their descriptions and drawings they did not always fail when they *surpassed* nature.

17 February 1860, Journal *XIII:149–51*

THE EARLIEST WILLOWS are now in the gray, too advanced to be silvery,—mouse or maltese-cat color.

26 March 1860, Journal *XIII:232*

I SEE A WOODCHUCK in the middle of the field at Assabet Bath. . . . He is very wary, every minute pausing and raising his head, and sometimes sitting erect and looking around. He is evidently nibbling some green thing, maybe clover. He runs at last, with an undulating motion, jerking his lumbering body along, and then stops when near a hole. But on the whole he runs and stops and looks round very much like a cat in the fields.

8 May 1860, Journal *XIII:283–84*

GEORGE MELVIN came to tell me this forenoon that a strange animal was killed on Sunday, the 9th, near the north line of the town, and it was not known certainly what it was. From his description I judged it to be a Canada lynx. . . .

Some weeks ago a little girl named Buttrick, who was huckleberrying near where the lynx was killed, was frightened by a wild animal leaping out of the bushes near her—*over* her, as she said—and bounding off. But no one then regarded her story. Also a Mr. Grimes, who lives in Concord just on the line, tells me that some month ago he heard from his house the loud cry of an animal in the woods northward, and told his wife that if he were in Canada he should say it was a bob-tailed cat. He had lived seven years in Canada and seen a number of this kind of animal.

11 September 1860, Journal *XIV:78*

SO WITH THE FRUIT of the burdock . . . both men and animals, apparently such as have shaggy coats, are employed in transporting them. I have even relieved a cat with a large mass of them which she could not get rid of, and I frequently see a cow with a bunch in the end of her whisking tail, with which, perhaps, she stings herself in her vain efforts to brush off imagined flies.

"The Dispersion of Seeds," Faith in a Seed, *97-98*

WE HAVE A KITTEN a third grown which often carries its tail almost flat on its back like a squirrel.

20 October 1860, Journal *XIV:161*

THESE TAWNY-WHITE OAKS are thus by their color and character the lions among trees, or rather, not to compare them with a foreign animal, they are the cougars or panthers—the American lions—among the trees, for nearly such is that of the cougar which walks beneath and amid or springs upon them. There is plainly this harmony between the color of our chief wild beast of the cat kind and our chief tree.

17 November 1860, Journal *XIV:250*

YOU WOULD SAY that some men had been tempted to live in this world at all only by the offer of a bounty by the general government—a bounty on living—to any one who will consent to be *out* at this era of the world, the object of the governors being to create a nursery for their navy. I told such a man the other day that I had got a Canada lynx here in Concord, and his instant question was, "Have you got the reward for him?" What reward? Why, the ten dollars which the State offers. As long as I saw him he neither said nor thought anything about the lynx, but only about this reward. "Yes," said he, "this State offers ten dollars reward." You might have inferred that ten dollars was something rarer in this neighborhood than a lynx even, and he was anxious to see it on that account. I have thought that a lynx was a bright-eyed, four-legged, furry beast of the cat kind, very *current*, indeed, though its natural gait is by leaps. But he knew it to be a draught drawn by the cashier of the wildcat bank on the State treasury, payable at sight. Then I reflected that the first money was of leather, or a whole creature (whence *pecunia*, from *pecus*, a herd), and, since leather was at first furry, I easily understood the connection between a lynx and ten dollars, and found that all money was traceable right back to the original wildcat bank. But the fact was that, instead of receiving ten dollars for the lynx which I had got, I had paid away some

dollars in order to get him. So, you see, I was away back in a
gray antiquity behind the institution of money,—further than
history goes. . . .

 . . . [T]hough money can buy no fine fruit whatever, and
we are never made truly rich by the possession of it, the value
of things generally is commonly estimated by the amount of
money they will fetch. A thing is not valuable—*e. g.* a fine situation for a house—until it is convertible into so much money,
that is, can cease to be what it is and become something else
which you prefer. So you will see that all prosaic people who
possess only the commonest sense, who believe strictly in this
kind of wealth, are speculators in fancy stocks and continually
cheat themselves, but poets and all discerning people, who have
an object in life and know what they want, speculate in real
values. The mean and low values of anything depend on it[s]
convertibility into something else—*i. e.* have nothing to do with
its intrinsic value.

29 November 1860, Journal *XIV:282–83*

A KITTEN is so flexible that she is almost double; the hind
parts are equivalent to another kitten with which the fore part
plays. She does not discover that her tail belongs to her till you
tread upon it.

How eloquent she can be with her tail! Its sudden swellings
and vibrations! She jumps into a chair and then stands on her
hind legs to look out the window; looks steadily at objects far
and near, first turning her gaze to this side then to that, for she
loves to look out a window as much as any gossip. Ever and
anon she bends back her ears to hear what is going on within
the room, and all the while her eloquent tail is reporting the
progress and success of her survey by speaking gestures which
betray her interest in what she sees.

Then what a delicate hint she can give with her tail! passing perhaps underneath, as you sit at table, and letting the tip of her tail just touch your legs, as much as to say, I am here and ready for that milk or meat, though she may not be so forward as to look round at you when she emerges.

Only skin-deep lies the feral nature of the cat, unchanged still. I just had the misfortune to rock on to our cat's leg, as she was lying playfully spread out under my chair. Imagine the sound that arose, and which was excusable; but what will you say to the fierce growls and flashing eyes with which she met me for a quarter of an hour thereafter? No tiger in its jungle could have been savager.

15 February 1861, Journal *XIV:314–15*

IT IS AMUSING TO OBSERVE how a kitten regards the attic, kitchen, or shed where it was bred as its castle to resort to in time of danger. It loves best to sleep on some elevated place, as a shelf or chair, and for many months does not venture far from the back door where it first saw the light. Two rods is a great range for it, but so far it is tempted, when the dew is off, by the motions of grasshoppers and crickets and other such small game, sufficiently novel and surprising to it. They frequently have a wheezing cough, which some refer to grasshoppers' wings across their windpipes. The kitten has been eating grasshoppers.

If some member of the household with whom they are familiar—their mistress or master—goes forth into the garden, they are then encouraged to take a wider range, and for a short season explore the more distant bean and cabbage rows, or, if several of the family go forth at once,—as it were a reconnaissance in force,—the kitten does a transient scout duty outside, but yet on the slightest alarm they are seen bounding back with great leaps over the grass toward the castle, where they stand panting on the door-step, with their small lower jaws fallen, until they fill up with courage again. A cat looks down with complacency on the strange dog from the corn-barn window.

The kitten when it is two or three months old is full of play. Ever and anon she takes up her plaything in her mouth and carries it to another place,—a distant corner of the room or some other nook, as under a rocker,—or perchance drops it at your feet, seeming to delight in the mere carriage of it, as if it were her prey—tiger-like. In proportion to her animal spirits are her quick motions and sudden whirlings about on the carpet or in the air. She may make a great show of scratching and biting, but let her have your hand and she will presently lick it instead.

They are so naturally stealthy, skulking and creeping about, affecting holes and darkness, that they will enter a shed rather by some hole under the door-sill than go over the sill through the open door.

Though able to bear cold, few creatures love warmth more or sooner find out where the fire is. The cat, whether she comes home wet or dry, directly squeezes herself under the cooking-stove, and stews her brain there, if permitted. If the cat is in the kitchen, she is most likely to be found under the stove.

[May–October?] 1861, Journal *XIV:340–42*

FOUR LITTLE KITTENS just born; lay like stuffed skins of kittens in a heap, with pink feet; so flimsy and helpless they lie, yet blind, without any stiffness or ability to stand. . . .

The kitten can already spit at a fortnight old, and it can mew from the first, though it often makes the motion of mewing without uttering any sound.

The cat about to bring forth seeks out some dark and secret place for the purpose, not frequented by other cats.

The kittens' ears are at first nearly concealed in the fur, and at a fortnight old they are mere broad-based triangles with a side foremost. But the old cat is ears for them at present, and comes running hastily to their aid when she hears them mew and licks them into contentment again. Even at three weeks the kitten cannot fairly walk, but only creeps feebly with outspread legs. But thenceforth its ears visibly though gradually lift and sharpen themselves.

At three weeks old the kitten begins to walk in a staggering and creeping manner and even to play a little with its mother, and, if you put your ear close, you may hear it purr. It is remarkable that it will not wander far from the dark corner where the cat has left it, but will instinctively find its way back to it, probably by the sense of touch, and will rest nowhere else. Also it is careful not to venture too near the edge of a precipice, and its claws are ever extended to save itself in such places. It washes itself somewhat, and assumes many of the attitudes of an old cat at this age. By the disproportionate size of its feet and head and legs now it reminds you [of] a lion.

I saw it scratch its ear to-day, probably for the first time; yet it lifted one of its hind legs and scratched its ear as effectually as an old cat does. So this is instinctive, and you may say that, when a kitten's ear first itches, Providence comes to the rescue and lifts its hind leg for it. You would say that this little creature was as perfectly protected by its instinct in its infancy as an old man can be by his wisdom. I observed when she first noticed the figures on the carpet, and also put up her paws to touch or play with surfaces a foot off. By the same instinct that they find the mother's teat before they can see they scratch their ears and guard against falling.

[*September–October*] *1861,* Journal *XIV:344–45*

IN SHORT, all good things are wild and free. . . . Give me for my friends and neighbors wild men, not tame ones. The wildness of the savage is but a faint symbol of the awful ferity with which good men and lovers meet.

I love even to see the domestic animals reassert their native rights,—any evidence that they have not wholly lost their original wild habits and vigor; as when my neighbor's cow breaks out of her pasture early in the spring and boldly swims the river. . . .

Any sportiveness in cattle is unexpected. I saw one day a herd of a dozen bullocks and cows running about and frisking in unwieldy sport, like huge rats, even like kittens. They shook their heads, raised their tails, and rushed up and down a hill, and I perceived by their horns, as well as by their activity, their relation to the deer tribe. But, alas! a sudden loud *Whoa!* would have damped their ardor at once, reduced them from venison to beef, and stiffened their sides and sinews like the locomotive. Who but the Evil One has cried "Whoa!" to mankind? Indeed, the life of cattle, like that of many men, is but a sort of locomotiveness; they move a side at a time, and man, by his machinery, is meeting the horse and the ox half-way. Whatever part the whip has touched is thenceforth palsied. Who would ever think of a *side* of any of the supple cat tribe, as we speak of a *side* of beef?

"*Walking*," Excursions and Poems, *234–35*

A NOTE ON TEXTS

For nearly a century the standard edition has been *The Writings of Henry David Thoreau*, edited by Bradford Torrey and Francis H. Allen, 20 volumes (Boston: Houghton Mifflin, 1906), volumes VII to XX of which comprise the *Journal* (separately numbered I to XIV). The 1906 Houghton Mifflin edition is being superseded by the ongoing *The Writings of Henry D. Thoreau* (Princeton, N.J.: Princeton University Press, 1971–), which among other titles has published seven volumes of the *Journal* to date. The Princeton edition of the *Journal* prints Thoreau's text exactly as it appears in manuscript and retains all peculiarities of his spelling, punctuation, and syntax. The Spirit of Thoreau series makes occasional editorial interpolations— indicated by square brackets—for cases in which the Princeton literal transcription might cause confusion and to provide context for certain passages. Arabic numerals indicate the seven volumes of the Princeton edition; roman numerals, the volumes of the 1906 *Journal* not yet superseded by Princeton.

FURTHER READING

Works by Thoreau

❦ *Cape Cod.* Edited by Joseph J. Moldenhauer. Princeton: Princeton University Press, 1988.

❦ *The Correspondence of Henry David Thoreau.* Edited by Walter Harding and Carl Bode. New York: New York University Press, 1958. Reprint, Westport, Conn.: Greenwood, 1974.

❦ *Excursions and Poems.* Edited by Bradford Torrey and Francis H. Allen. Boston, Houghton Mifflin, 1906.

❦ *Faith in a Seed: The Dispersion of Seeds and Other Late Natural History Writings.* Edited by Bradley P. Dean. Washington, D.C.: Island Press, 1993.

❦ *The Journal of Henry David Thoreau.* Volumes I–XIV. Edited by Bradford Torrey and Francis H. Allen. 1906. Reprint, Boston: Houghton Mifflin, 1949.

❦ *Journal.* Volumes 1–6, 8. Elizabeth Hall Witherell, editor-in-chief. Princeton: Princeton University Press, 1981–2002.

❦ *The Maine Woods.* Edited by Joseph J. Moldenhauer. Princeton: Princeton University Press, 1972.

❦ *Reform Papers.* Edited by Wendell Glick. Princeton: Princeton University Press, 1973.

❦ *Thoreau's Fact Book in the Harry Elkins Widener Collection in the Harvard College Library.* Facsimile edition by Kenneth Walter Cameron. 3 volumes. Hartford, Conn.: Transcendental Books, 1966.

❦ *Walden.* Edited by J. Lyndon Shanley. Princeton: Princeton University Press, 1971.

❦ *A Week on the Concord and Merrimack Rivers.* Edited by Carl F. Hovde, William L. Howarth, and Elizabeth Hall Witherell. Princeton: Princeton University Press, 1980.

Further Reading

Other Works Cited and Secondary Sources

❧ Alcott, Louisa May. *Little Women.* 2 volumes. Boston: Roberts, 1868, 1869.

❧ American Kennel Club. *The Complete Dog Book.* 19th edition. New York: Howell Book House, 1997.

❧ Caras, Roger. *A Cat Is Watching: A Look at the Way Cats See Us.* New York: Simon & Schuster, 1989.

❧ Channing, William Ellery. *Thoreau, the Poet-Naturalist* (1873). New edition, enlarged. Edited by F. B. Sanborn. Boston: Charles E. Goodspeed, 1902.

❧ Dale-Green, Patricia. *Cult of the Cat.* Boston: Houghton Mifflin, 1963. Republished as *The Archetypal Cat.* Dallas: Spring Publications, 1983.

❧ Derr, Mark. *Dog's Best Friend: Annals of the Dog-Human Relationship.* New York: Henry Holt, 1997.

❧ Emerson, Edward Waldo. *Emerson in Concord.* Boston: Houghton Mifflin, 1888.

❧ ———. *Henry Thoreau as Remembered by a Young Friend.* Boston: Houghton Mifflin, 1917.

❧ Emerson, Ellen Tucker. *The Life of Lidian Jackson Emerson.* Edited by Delores Bird Carpenter. Boston: Twayne, 1980.

❧ Emerson, Ralph Waldo. *The Letters of Ralph Waldo Emerson.* 10 volumes. Edited by Ralph L. Rusk and Eleanor M. Tilton. New York: Columbia University Press, 1939, 1990–95.

❧ Fiennes, Richard and Alice. *The Natural History of Dogs.* Garden City, N.Y.: Natural History Press, 1970.

❧ Fogle, Bruce. *The Encyclopedia of the Cat.* New York: DK Publishing, 1997.

❧ ———. *The Encyclopedia of the Dog.* New York: DK Publishing, 1995.

❧ ———. editor. *Interrelations between People and Pets.* Springfield, Ill.: Charles C. Thomas, 1981.

Further Reading

🐾 Follen, Eliza Lee (Cabot). *True Stories About Dogs and Cats*. Boston: Whittemore, Niles, & Hall, 1855.

🐾 Katcher, Aaron Honori, and Alan M. Beck, editors. *New Perspectives on Our Lives with Companion Animals*. Philadelphia: University of Pennsylvania Press, 1983.

🐾 Masson, Jeffrey Moussaieff. *Dogs Never Lie about Love: Reflections on the Emotional World of Dogs*. New York: Crown Publishers, 1997.

🐾 Morris, Desmond. *Cat World: A Feline Encyclopedia*. New York: Penguin Reference, 1997.

🐾 Rogers, Katharine M. *The Cat and the Human Imagination: Feline Images from Bast to Garfield*. Ann Arbor: University of Michigan Press, 1998.

🐾 Sattelmeyer, Robert. *Thoreau's Reading: A Study in Intellectual History with Bibliographical Catalogue*. Princeton: Princeton University Press, 1988.

🐾 Schwartz, Marion. *A History of Dogs in the Early Americas*. New Haven: Yale University Press, 1997.

🐾 Serpell, James. *In the Company of Animals: A Study of Human-Animal Relationships*. Oxford: Basil Blackwell, 1986.

🐾 Shaftesbury, Anthony, Earl of. *Characteristics of Men, Manners, Opinions, Times*. Volumes I–II (1711). Edited by John M. Robertson. Indianapolis: Bobbs-Merrill, 1964.

🐾 Thomas, Elizabeth Marshall. *The Hidden Life of Dogs*. Boston: Houghton Mifflin, 1993.

🐾 ———. *The Social Lives of Dogs: The Grace of Canine Company*. New York: Simon & Schuster, 2000.

🐾 ———. *The Tribe of Tiger: Cats and Their Culture*. New York: Simon & Schuster, 1994.

🐾 Topsell, Edward. *The History of Four-footed Beasts*. 1607. Reprint of 1658 edition, New York: Da Capo Press, 1967.

🐾 Van Vechten, Carl. *The Tiger in the House*. New York: Alfred A. Knopf, 1920.

THE SPIRIT OF THOREAU

"How many a man has dated a new era in his life from the reading of a book," wrote Henry David Thoreau in *Walden*. Today that book, perhaps more than any other American work, continues to provoke, inspire, and change lives all over the world, and each rereading is fresh and challenging. Yet as Thoreau's countless admirers know, there is more to the man than *Walden*. An engineer, poet, teacher, naturalist, lecturer, and political activist, he truly had several more lives to lead, and each one speaks forcefully to us today.

The Spirit of Thoreau introduces the thoughts of a great writer on a variety of important topics, some that we readily associate him with, some that may be surprising. Each book includes selections from his familiar published works as well as from less well known and recently discovered lectures, letters, and journal entries. Thoreau claimed that "to read well, that is, to read true books in a true spirit, is a noble exercise, and one that will task the reader more than any exercise which the customs of the day esteem." The volume editors and the Thoreau Society believe that you will find these new aspects of Thoreau an exciting "exercise" indeed.

The Thoreau Society is honored to bring you these titles in cooperation with the University of Massachusetts Press. The publisher of many important studies of Thoreau and other Transcendentalists, the press is also widely recognized for its outstanding titles on several aspects of New England culture.

You are invited to continue exploring Thoreau by joining our society. For more than sixty years we have presented publications, annual gatherings, and other programs to further the appreciation of

The Spirit of Thoreau

Thoreau's thought and writings. In ways that the author of *Walden* could not have imagined, his message is still changing lives in a brand-new era.

For membership information, write to The Thoreau Society, 55 Old Bedford Road, Concord, Massachusetts 01742; call 978-369-5310; or visit our website www.thoreausociety.org.

Wesley T. Mott
Series Editor
The Thoreau Society

WESLEY T. MOTT
is professor of English at Worcester Polytechnic Institute
and an editor of the *Journal* for the Princeton Thoreau Edition.

ELIZABETH MARSHALL THOMAS
is an anthropologist, novelist, and best-selling author
of books about dogs and cats.